Children of Alcoholics: A Guidebook for Educators, Therapists, and Parents

Robert J. Ackerman
Western Michigan University

LEARNING PUBLICATIONS
Holmes Beach, Florida

Library of Congress Card Number: 78-55067

Learning Publications, Inc.
PO Box 1326
Holmes Beach, Florida   33509

Hardcover ISBN 0-918452-06-6

Softcover ISBN 0-918452-07-4

Cover Design by Rob Gutek

Printing: 1 2 3 4 5 6 7 8   Year: 8 9 0 1 2

Printed and bound in the United States of America

to
my Mother and Father
who know that love is a verb

ACKNOWLEDGEMENTS

The writing of this book depended on the contributions of many people. I cannot thank them all. However, I wish to give special thanks to Pamela Johnson Ackerman who encouraged and advised me in this endeavor from its origin to the reality of the final page.

A special thanks goes to Shirley and Howard McFadden for their work among families of alcoholics, and Wilma F. Busse and Sharon L. Surratt. I have learned a great deal from them. I would also like to express my appreciation for the support of Leila Bradfield, Robert M. Brashear, Edsel L. Erickson, Robert M. Oswald, Morton O. Wagenfeld, and Thomas K. Williams. They shared with me many of their ideas and experiences.

In addition, I am indebted to Penne Ferguson and Barbara McFadden for administrative support and to Ruth Burkett Park for her editorial assistance. They have my sincere appreciation.

Finally, my heartfelt thanks goes to the parents and their children with whom I have worked. From our pain and accomplishments I hope that I have learned enough so that this book contributes to a better life for those who follow.

TABLE OF CONTENTS

PART A

THE CHILD OF AN ALCOHOLIC: WHAT IT'S LIKE

1

The Reality of Unseen Casualties

In the United States today alcoholism ranks as one of this country's most serious health threats, yet it is one of the most neglected conditions in our society. None, however, are more neglected than the "unseen casualties" of alcoholism—the children of alcoholic parents. This condition has been allowed to develop due to such reasons as the inability to accurately estimate the extent of alcoholism in our society, myths and generalizations like "alcoholics are skid row individuals," and the ambiguity with which most Americans view alcohol use and problems that arise from it.

It is seldom realized that alcohol can be an "equal opportunity destroyer." (Ackerman, 1977) In fact, according to the Schaffer Commission Report of 1972, less than forty percent of Americans considered alcohol as a drug. There are an estimated nine million alcoholics in the United States today. (National Council on Alcoholism, 1977) Of these nine million, only three to five percent represent the stereotypic skid row concept. The so-called "average" alcoholic is a man or woman with a good home, job, and family. Alcoholics are, in reality, our neighbors, our friends, and the parents of some of the children in our classrooms.

Statistics concerning alcoholism are truly startling. It ranks with heart disease, cancer, and mental illness as one of the four biggest national health problems. It accounts directly or indirectly for forty percent of the problems brought to family courts. According to a recent economic cost analysis, alcoholism costs our country more than thirty-one billion dollars a year. (Berry, 1977)

It is interesting, however, that while many statistics are cited regarding the impact of alcoholism on society, the emotional impact on individuals is rarely mentioned. There are an estimated twenty-seven million children of alcoholics in this country. Of these twenty-seven million, twenty million are of adolescent or preadolescent age. (Hornik, 1974) Not only is this fact often overlooked, but also the children themselves are truly "forgotten children." (Cork, 1969)

Many of these youngsters are seen during their school years by numerous institutions and agencies, but it is seldom that their environmental circumstances are examined for detrimental influences. For some children, the effects of environment are minimal; for many others, however, undesirable influences may be quite detrimental. Unfortunately, these influences are seldom dealt with, or at best are noticed only indirectly.

The institution that sees children of alcoholics the most, and that could have a significant impact on many of them, is the school. The purpose of this book is not to get the school involved in treating alcoholics, but rather to explore the parameters by which the school and its personnel may be able to help minimize the effects of alcoholism in the home on many of its youngest victims.

THE ALCOHOLIC FAMILY

Alcoholism affects the entire family. Because it subjects all members of a household to constant stress and fears of various kinds, it has often been referred to as a "family illness." In most situations, the family members get little attention until the "primary patient" desires help or is forced to get help. At this point, the alcoholic is the primary consideration, and family members are at best secondary.

Many alcoholics do not get help. They continue their drinking; and under the primary patient philosophy, the other family members will never be seen or considered.

It is not necessary, however, for an alcoholic to receive help in order for family members to be considered and helped. Perhaps the roles should be reversed so that the family would be considered "primary" and the alcoholic "secondary." This might upset a lot of alcohol treatment-oriented individuals, but merely treating the alcoholic cannot encompass all the effects of alcoholism. What is needed is the concept of and eventual programs for "family recovery."

Statistically, most families suffering from alcoholism are intact as a two-parent family, and currently the alcoholic in the majority of cases is the father. This is true for several reasons. In the first place, there are more male alcoholics than female alcoholics, with the ratio falling somewhere between four to one or six to one. Secondly, the majority of wives of alcoholics who have children tend to stay with the male alcoholic. In fact, some statistics state that ninety percent of such women remain with their husbands. On the other hand, only a few males who are married to a female alcoholic will remain with her, perhaps as few as ten percent. Thus it is seen that societal reactions to alcoholism are deeply dependent upon the sex of the alcoholic. Clearly, the double standard is evident. This ratio, however, may soon change, as womens' roles are changing and the female alcoholic is not hidden by society, as previously was the case.

If a woman is married, has children, and happens to be an alcoholic, one of the first things to be said about her, upon discovery of the alcoholism, is that she is an "unfit" mother. On the other hand, rarely is it initially said of the male alcoholic that he is an "unfit" father.

Stages of Adjustment

The plight of the typical family of an alcoholic father can be illustrated by examining the stages of adjustment attempted by the wife and other family members. (Jackson, 1954)

1.   The first stage involves family attempts to deny that a problem exists. At this point the alcoholic is drinking excessively, may be spending a great deal of time away from home, missing work, and possibly having some monetary problems. Additionally, the father's increasingly sporadic alcohol-related behavior is beginning to place a great deal of strain on family relationships. However, the mother has developed a pattern of covering up for the father. She makes excuses for his job absenteeism and rationalizes explanations to the children's frequent question, "where's Daddy?" Essentially, she is drawn into a pattern of denial which is critical for the alcoholic to maintain in order to keep drinking. On one hand, the wife is forced to defend his behavior; on the other, she has no effective positive

means to initiate new behavior. This first stage is also characterized by periods of sobriety on the part of the alcoholic, in which all seems to be normal. These periods are part of the denying process; since both partners have pledged to be ideal mates, they must continue to try to convince themselves that no problem exists. Eventually it becomes obvious to the wife that all is not well, that the drinking in their family is different from that in other families. Now the scene is set for the second stage of attempts to eliminate the problem.

2.   The second stage is characterized by two types of approaches by nonalcoholic members of the family: verbal and behavioral. They are in essence "home remedies." The verbal approach consists of attempts to reason with the alcoholic in hopes of arriving at a logical decision to quit drinking. When the wife's efforts to reason with her husband fail, hope gives way to bitterness and the verbal approach then takes on tones of emotional pleas, demands of promises, threats, and morality lectures. The behavioral aspects include such things as the family going through social disengagement. To avoid embarrassing situations, the family quits accepting and giving social invitations. The children no longer have their friends over for fear of embarrassment or unpredictable behavior. The wife, and perhaps other family members, may also try such tactics as pouring the alcohol out, not buying any more, or locking it up.

The home remedies, whatever they are, all have one thing in common—which is that they usually do not work.

3.   Stage three is one of disorganization. It is marked by a "what's the use" attitude. The family has come to regard the problem as permanent. The mother feels unloved, helpless to be a "good wife," and unable to meet family needs. The children are beginning to feel rejected by both parents, and the family is quite effectively disorganized emotionally.

4.   In the fourth stage, there is an attempt to reorganize in spite of the problems. It is an effort to keep the family unit together and to try to function as normally as possible. At this stage the nonalcoholic spouse finds it necessary to step in and assume many of the duties and responsibilities formerly belonging to the alcoholic. As a means of coping, the wife and the children systematically and gradually begin to exclude the alcoholic from their lives.

5.   The fifth stage involves efforts to escape the problem by making a decision to physically separate from the alcoholic. The problems at this point are too severe to endure and a separation is desired. Although separations do occur, as was mentioned earlier, statistically it is most likely that the mother and the children will stay. If they

do leave, they are faced with other problems such as relocation, economic security, care of small children, and numerous other considerations. All of this may be further complicated by the presence of the alcoholic or physical threats of violence if the family should leave. Also, if the wife has begun to adopt the ideas of alcoholism as an illness or disease, she may find herself caught in an ethical conflict. To separate from a man who is simply violent and dangerous is more acceptable than to separate from a man who is suffering from a serious illness.

6. In case the wife and offspring decide to leave, the final step is the reorganization of the one-parent family. At this point it is necessary for further reshuffling of family roles and responsibilities. It is obvious that this stage does not eliminate all the stress for the family. It may only cause stress in other situations.

7. In a few cases, the last step is more positive. If the alcoholic father chooses to give up drinking, the entire family is reorganized for a fresh start. This stage holds pitfalls because after the husband's sobriety has been obtained and perhaps maintained for a time, the family expects to enter "paradise." But difficulties will continue to exist, as they do in all families. Difficulties which were formerly believed to be related to the father's drinking may surface as ordinary, normal, family disagreements. Acceptance of the sober alcoholic is not automatic. Since during all of the

previous stages short term periods of sobriety were experienced, the wife and the children are apt to maintain a "wait and see" attitude.

At this point, one of two possible conditions may develop. One possible condition is that even though the alcoholic actually quits drinking, results of the previous breakdown in family communications continue to take their toll on the emotions of family members. In this instance the alcohol is gone, but the wife cannot forget the pains and emotional stress caused in the past by her husband's alcoholism. She and the children continue to feel bitter, fearful, and insecure. The opposite situation that can accompany cessation of the father's drinking is that the family finds new unity and strength for growth. If the wife has developed understanding of her own problems as well as her husband's, she can help the entire family to recognize that sobriety alone may not be enough and that there are needs to be met for all members of the family.

The above stages of family adjustment to an alcoholic father illustrate various adaptations that a family typically experiences when there is an alcoholic parent. Use of a male alcoholic in the example was not intended to ignore women alcoholics, but to outline the development of a familiar pattern in our society. Throughout the remainder of the book a distinction as to the sex of the alcoholic will not be specific. The real purpose of this book is to raise the level of awareness of the plight of the other family members. Throughout all of these stages, the family is forced to adapt to constant change. Whether or not a family goes through several or all of the stages, one characteristic is evident. The children are present, and they must be considered.

Family Interrelationships

What are the effects of all this adaptation and change? Many alcoholics are not aware of the emotional hazards they unthinkingly cause for their young. These effects, if considered at all, are seen as latent in the home, but may be seen as manifest by others outside the home. In order to consider the impact of these effects, some of the dynamics occurring in the home should be noted.

It is critical to consider whether or not both parents are alcoholic. In cases where both parents are involved in alcoholism, physical as well as emotional needs of the children may be unmet. When parents are unable or unwilling to assist in the home, their children may be consistently forced to organize and run the household. They may be picking up after parents and assuming extremely mature roles for their ages.

Time of onset of parental alcoholism is also an important consideration. Were the children born into an alcoholic home, or did parental addiction occur later in their life—and at what age? It is fairly well agreed upon in various educational researches that the impacts of emotional crises upon children are more detrimental at some ages than at others. Many children will experience an emotional separation from their parents, often feeling rejected by both parents even though only one is alcoholic. Lack of emotional security, and inability to discriminate between love as a noun and love as a verb, take their toll on many children of irresponsible parents. Alcoholic behavior in the family can prohibit intimate involvement and clearly impede the development of essential family bonds. When children's emotional needs have been stunted by neglect or destroyed by cruelty, the traditional image of parents as mentors and guides for their offspring becomes a farce. Clearly, the generally agreed upon significance of the positive influence of parents in the early education of children becomes questionable. (Brookover and Erickson, 1975) It cannot be assumed that the proper parental roles towards education are being met, let along attempted, in the alcoholic home.

The rolls their parents play in the family are of critical importance in the development of children. When a parent is alcoholic, parental roles are too often marked by inconsistency; and inconsistency is exhibited by both the alcoholic and the nonalcoholic parent. The alcoholic parent behaves like several different individuals with conflicting reactions and unpredictable attitudes. Often his or her role performance is dictated by successive periods of drunken behavior, remorse or guilt followed by high degrees of anxiety and tension, and finally, complete sobriety. Children may learn through experience to adapt themselves to such role inconsistency and even to develop some form of predictability; but little emotional security is found. What emotional security is available is usually obtainable only during periods of sobriety, and then only if other family issues are not producing tension.

A typical example of this kind of cycle goes as follows. On Friday night and all day Saturday the alcoholic is drunk. Sunday and Monday are hangover or recovery days, commonly marked by some degree of guilt or remorse. The middle of the week is the most normal. As the next weekend approaches, the alcoholic is being dominated by increasing anxiety and tension precipitating another drinking episode. The children in such a situation learn that whatever is needed, physically or emotionally, must be obtained in the middle of the week. These become the "gettin" days when the getting may be more optimal because it is at this time, if any, that parenting or positive stroking by the alcoholic will occur. This is also the time that many unrealistic as well as realistic promises are made, which may or may not be kept. Normal promises made on good days may go unfulfilled because the collection day is one of inebriation. Sometimes this results in the making of still bigger and more elaborate promises, which are in turn broken. Occasions when promises are kept are sporadic, so cannot be relied on, again adding to the inconsistency. The alcoholic may show exaggerated concern or love one day and mistreat the child the next day. It is little wonder that a major problem for such children is a lack of trust and security in relationships to an alcoholic parent.

The nonalcoholic parent is hampered in attempting to fulfill the needs of the children because he or she is usually under constant tension over what is happening or may happen. Even when the alcoholic is sober, the spouse tends to suspect that the situation is tenuous, and consequently cannot support the alcoholic's attempts to win respect and approval—knowing that the probability of consistency is low. The nonalcoholic parent, who is subjected to and controlled by the inconsistent nature of the alcoholic, may become so engrossed in trying to fulfill two roles that he or she is unable to fulfill one role adequately with any type of consistency. Just as the alcoholic fluctuates between different levels of sobriety and emotionalism, so does the nonalcoholic parent react to these positions. As a result, the nonalcoholic parent may be just as guilty as the alcoholic in showing too much concern for the children at times and too little at other times. In addition, the spouse, worried about the effects of alcoholic behavior in the family situation, is apt to become too protective of or fearful for the children. This protection is often misunderstood by the children, especially when it is negatively administered in the form of warnings against certain places or people, without explanation.

Perhaps much of the nonalcoholic spouse's parental concern is justified by the fact that as many as forty to sixty percent of children of alcoholic parents become alcoholics themselves. (Hindman, 1975) Much has been written about the causal factors for this phenomenon. The question is centered on the nature-nuture controversy surrounding alcoholism. Is alcoholism genetically hereditary or are other factors present? This author believes that the nuturing aspects play the more prominent role and that the damage inflicted on the child is not limited to preadolescence or adolescence, but has long-range implications.

Although not directly related to drinking practices, additional evidence that the nuture impact is the stronger influence is shown by the fact that children of alcoholic parents are more affected by the disharmony and rejection in the home life than by the drinking. They see that drinking stops once in a while, while the fighting and tension continues. This constant state of agitation affects personality development. More particularly, the child observes the use of alcohol as a method of dealing with uncomfortable situations. Although the child may vow not to drink and is cognizant of the potential harm of alcohol abuse, this position may give way to use of drinking as a means of escape during real or perceived crises in later life.

The two-parent family in which alcoholism affects one or both partners cannot provide a healthy parental relationship. A single, nonalcoholic parent can give children a healthier atmosphere. In a family where one of the parents is alcoholic, the other parent will not be able to singly overcome all of the impacts of the others' drinking; he or she cannot provide a separate environment because both parental roles are distorted or inconsistent. The nonalcoholic parent devotes energy in trying to deal with the alcoholic at various phases of adaptation, leaving little energy for the needs of the offspring. Often the children are forced into a position of increased responsibilities and unfamiliar roles. The eldest child may be put in charge of smaller children or be drawn into the role of confidant for the nonalcoholic spouse.

Sometimes children find themselves abandoned in the middle or forced to choose sides, either of which can lead to withdrawal and a preference to be left alone. It was earlier mentioned that family disengagement from contact with others is a form of adapting behavior to the alcoholic problem. Disengagement can also occur within the family itself. The children avoid family contact as often as possible, having learned that minimal contact may also mean minimal discomfort. Such children want only to be left alone. They no longer feel close to either parent. The need to be isolated from their parents' conflicts may carry over to their attitudes toward other adults. Such children associate solitude with absence of conflict; thus being alone is not always as feared as we might expect; it may be viewed as a pleasant time of relaxation.

Affection or emotional support outside the home is a vital aspect in helping such children. It will be considered in subsequent chapters.

Sometimes another major concern of parental roles is the problem of readaptation to the event of recovery by the alcoholic. Although the alcoholic may no longer be drinking, unless this readaptive process is successful and the family can establish and grow as a unit, the family may find itself on a "dry drunk," with most conditions in the family remaining the same as when the alcoholic was drinking. In such cases tension, anxiety, and conflict persist because other problems have not been solved. This situation is especially complicated if the family had expected all problems to disappear with cessation of drinking. What has failed to be realized is that normal family problems, which during the drinking years had been attributed to alcoholism, will continue to occur. The family needs to understand that throughout the drinking period family relationships were deteriorating or were never sufficiently established. Some children in the "dry drunk" situation are unable to remember anything but drinking behavior on the part of one or both parents. The recovering alcoholic may, in fact, be trying to parent properly, but since this is a new or strange behavior, it may not be entirely trusted within the family when drinking stops. The family must be incorporated in a new adaptive process. To ignore the role of the family in helping the recovering alcoholic support his or her sobriety, is to ignore the emotional impact that alcoholism has had on the family.

Many families can become recovered, or recovering, families. Many will not without assistance from others. Outside support becomes critical to this process, especially when we remember that there may be no support from within the family. Often children need help in acquiring or regaining a sense of trust in their parents and others.

Also vital to the children is the acquisition of self-awareness and self-esteem. Basic to a family recovery program is the question of whether the children can grow up to face life successfully. Will they be able to achieve a sense of security, to be able to grow while accepting their circumstances, and more importantly, to feel good about themselves?

When working with the children of alcoholic parents, alcoholism (and not just the alcoholic) should be addressed. The entire picture can be brought into focus and invisible symptoms, as well as easily-observed ones, can be discussed.

2

The Children: Their World and Their Preceptions

Not all children of alcoholic parents suffer identical emotional effects; in fact, some seem to survive quite well. Accounting for this are a variety of factors, such as age of onset of parental alcoholism, number of children in the family, ordinal position, friends outside of the family, and which parent is the alcoholic. However, it appears that of the studies involving these children, we can generalize into two broad categories, the "haves" and the "have nots." *What they have or do not have is an ability within themselves to establish positive primary relationships outside the home.*

The importance of the primary relationship for the development of a child is well established. It appears that although most primary relationships occur within the home, for many children of alcoholic parents these relationships are developed outside the home and are able to achieve virtually the same importance in the life of the child. Perhaps for the child of alcoholic parents it is not so important that primary relationships are established in the home, but that they are established somewhere. The issue of primary relationships becomes a determining factor. It will be further elaborated when addressing the role of the school and its personnel.

Although not all children of alcoholic parents are affected in the same way, there are some experiences (and, more particularly, reactions to these experiences) that all these children endure and share, regardless of the outcome of the experience. Many studies show that children in the "have not" category exhibit such problems as delinquency, anxiety, and depression. In addition, much research indicates that these youngsters may have poor self-concepts, are easily frustrated, perform poorly in school (probably due to the former characteristics), and are more likely to suffer adjustment problems. (Chafetz, 1971; Jackson, 1954; McKay, 1963; Nylander, 1958; Fine, 1975) What then do the children see and how do they feel about their situations that may contribute to such findings?

THE YOUNG WORLD

"We all just go off and nurse our wounds . . . nobody cares how you feel." (Cork, 1969) This statement made by a child of alcoholic parents, stated to Margaret Cork, reveals much insight into the unseen world of these children. The children possess opinions—often very clear opinions—about their situations and the behavior of their parents.

When such children discuss their parents to counselors, parental role inconsistency is a major theme. The same is true when parents are discussing their children. The only difference may be that the alcoholic is putting forth inconsistency and the children are forced to accept it, thus reacting to it in behavioral patterns that normal situations would not make necessary. The parents are actors and the children become reactors. Because they receive inconsistency, they are forced to react to it in ways that are consistent neither with their roles as children nor with their basic personalities.

Often children of alcoholics see themselves as extremely mature for their age. This is due to the fact that they are often called upon to act more grown-up than their parents. They must anticipate their reactions to the parents' actions and, therefore, limit and subjugate many childhood mannerisms. They consciously choose to curb their feelings and behavior in order "not to rock the boat." In essence, these children constantly monitor their own behavior, frequently at the expense of creating feelings of conflict, resentment, anxiety, and anger within themselves. Another reaction to these demands—one which causes

great stress for the children—is that of their own ambiva-
lence. They may find themselves loving the person who
drinks, but hating the drinking.

Children see parental behavior as a reflection of their
own worth. Children of alcoholics tend to feel that because
there is something wrong in their family, there is something wrong with them. In time, they begin to realize that
their home and their family are different from those of
their friends. In their homes, (unlike in normal ones), family relationships and functions are regulated by the condition of the alcoholic. It becomes difficult for children to
return to their own homes after being in their friends'
homes, experiencing "normal" family relationships. This
difficulty is further compounded by the fact that the family, as described in Chapter One, may be attempting to
deny, cover up, or eliminate the problem without revealing
it to outside sources. Too often the thoughts and emotions
of such children remain unshared with friends, because on
the one hand they may be under orders from their nonalcoholic parent to say nothing or to pretend; on the other
hand they may feel embarrassed and fearful that friends
cannot understand their predicament. Worse yet, they may
fear ridicule or rejection from friends. Even within the
home, siblings may isolate themselves, instead of sharing
feelings of mutual endurance. Much of children's modeling
behavior is taken from their parents, and it should be of no

surprise that the children of alcoholic parents often argue more than others, thus finding little psychological comfort from other brothers and sisters.

Sibling relationships are further complicated by the roles that may be placed upon individual brothers and sisters. In many cases the oldest child may be called upon to take a great deal of responsibility for the other children, which not only places role strain on the child, but also puts him or her in competition with the parent whose job the child is attempting to fill. The oldest may soon tire of the unwanted position and resent the feelings of the displaced parent as well as the feelings of his or her siblings.

Another uncomfortable situation occurs when the eldest becomes the constant source of ventilation and support for the nonalcoholic parent.

Outside the home, oldest children may experience role inconsistency when coming under the influence of other adults. In school, for example, they must revert back to their original role of adolescent, student, sophomore, etc., where a few hours before and few hours in the future they will again be faced with the responsibility of helping to raise the family of an alcoholic.

THE YOUNG OPINION

According to limited studies in this field, children of alcoholic parents have certain specific attitudes in common about alcoholism in the family.

One finding is that an alcoholic mother is regarded by children as more detrimental than an alcoholic father. Societal disapproval may play a large role here, as well as the obvious role of mother-child bonding and relationship. Research also indicates that in cases where the mother is alcoholic, there are more behavioral and emotional problems for the children. (Cork, 1969) Female alcoholics usually suffer more societal disdain and reaction than do male alcoholics. Also, the male traditionally has fewer hours of contact with the children, particularly when they are young.

Traditional roles could also affect how alcoholism is handled in the family. If the alcoholic is male, the tolerance level and at times even acceptability for his behavior will be relatively higher, and it will be endured for a longer period of time, than if the alcoholic is female.

Patterns of time that elapse during the process of becoming alcoholic vary according to sex. Currently in our society, the durations of time between social drinking, problem drinking, and alcoholism are shorter for women than for men. This phenomenon is not totally explainable, but certainly the societal reactions to the woman's drinking increases the amount of stress, anxiety, and perhaps guilt that the woman may be enduring.

Another fact revealed by studies is that children consider fighting in the home worse than the drinking it accompanies. The children can find some respite from the drinking, but not from the fighting and constant tension caused by alcoholism. One of the hardest problems for children is not the acceptance of parental drinking, but trying to understand the relationship between their parents. Unable to understand that it is a drug-affected relationship, they have difficulty understanding why their parents constantly argue or why they have little emotional involvement with each other. They are puzzled as to why the couple stays together; on the other hand, when separation occurs, what little security they have is shattered. The children's feelings are reflected in loss of sleep, feelings of hopelessness, and alienation from the family and from themselves; they feel totally powerless to make the situation disappear. They come to consider themselves pawns in a game which they do not understand, or victims of a battle they cannot escape.

Because of lack of family closeness, the children are deprived of normal family fun. There are few enjoyable activities because family life is structured around the alcohol problem, or avoided because of it, or ends up being influenced by it. Consequently, "have" children who are able to carry over primary relationships tend to seek outside activities and possible close contacts outside the immediate family. However, if a child is in the "have not" category, in which all primary relationships are stunted or absent, any outside relationships he or she forms will tend to be characterized by insecurity, fear, and a lack of trust in others. By holding back the giving and receiving of affection, "have nots" literally reject the thing that they desire. This holding back restricts the opportunities for outside fun, which makes it evident why many studies indicate that children of alcoholic parents have little involvement in community activities. Feelings of detachment and lack of trust in others leave such children with little peer support.

Another effect on attitudes of children of alcoholics derives from emotional abuse in the home. The youngsters are expected to endure many storms, with few opportunities for ventilation of their own feelings. The domination of parental alcoholism deprives them of the opportunity to cope with their own emotions.

Unfortunately, help is rarely accessible to these children. Because of limited programs and even more limited information on access to them, the children rarely seek help themselves. If any help is received, it usually comes as an indirect result of some other family problem or of a childs' own behavioral problems at school or elsewhere outside the home. Even then, such attention seldom discovers the actual family situation.

Alcoholics may move beyond emotional abuse to physical abuse as their involvement with drinking increases. The relationship between child abuse and alcoholism is an old one. Spouse beating also causes much suffering to children who must witness it, or who become drawn into the violence when coming to the aid of an abused parent.

The instinct to survive is strong in everyone. Children who feel abandoned, torn by conflict between parents, or helpless to cope with an alcoholic parent will attempt various methods of saving themselves. "Have not" children are apt to choose disassociation from the family and avoidance of close contacts with others. The "have" child is better able to form outside ties and to assume adult responsibilities, and this often brings admiration from neighbors, teachers, and peers who may not understand it as the by-product of a stressful situation. "Have" children may be extremely mature for their age; and since they are forced to do much for themselves and perhaps other family members, this ability spills over into other situations. However, these children are not seen as acting out their problems because "acting out" is usually considered as a negative behavior. In reality they may be acting out, but their actions are part of the "unseen casualty" syndrome. Children who overcompensate by growing up too soon bear their own kinds of scars inflicted by alcoholism in the home.

Studies indicate that parental drinking is most detrimental for children of six to seven, in early adolescence, and again in later adolescence. (Bosma, 1975) Family disengagement is accomplished by those children in all three age brackets who are able to discover mechanisms to achieve it. Children in late adolescence often see their solution as physical disengagement, and move out of the home environment if they possibly can. It is highly probable that many cases of educational dropout can be attributed to parental alcoholism.

This chapter began with the statement that the children of alcoholic parents feel no one cares, and this feeling is frequently carried over into school activities and social life outside the home. School and other involvement of youngsters go virtually unnoticed by parents who are absorbed by problems brought on by alcoholism. The children may feel that there are no parental expectations concerning how they do in school because as long as they are doing "OK"—which may be minimal—their activities are unnoticed.

3

Human Development and Personality Among Children of Alcoholics

Environment has a profound influence on physical, emotional, and personality development of children; in fact it is generally considered to be the dominating factor in human development.

Development is seen to reflect either biological or environmental influences which result in changes in the structure, thought, or behavior of a person. (Craig, 1976) Biological development involves processes of physical growth, aging, and maturation while environmental development involves circumstances surrounding an individual, with which he or she interacts emotionally and socially to form an individual personality structure. Obviously, human development is a blend of these two influences and their interreactions.

Analyzing the human development patterns of children are many schools of thought, of which Piaget, Freud,

Skinner, Maslow, Mead, and Sullivan are typical examples. Constant to these various models is the analysis of human development from the perspective of a "normal" or ideal type with normal growth patterns or stages serving as models.

In the case of children of alcoholics, however, levels of development may not always be normal. Children of alcoholics are apt to encounter developmental aspects with environmental implications different from those met by the child of nonalcoholic parents. Some of these differences will have detrimental effects; others will not. In individual cases it is not possible to predict which will or will not, since each child's development is unique and dependent upon a building-block theory of internalizing experiences. Not all experiences are equally recorded by different children. This chapter will attempt to raise some of the developmental concerns for children of alcoholics regarding physical, emotional, and personality considerations.

PHYSICAL DEVELOPMENT

Developmental concerns for children of alcoholic parents begin at the prenatal stage. Whether the child is born of an alcoholic mother or lives with an alcoholic father, detrimental aspects are present in the environment.

In the case of an alcoholic mother, the "fetal alcohol syndrome" can develop. (Jones, Smith, Ulleland, Streissgoth, 1973) This syndrome results in the physical underdevelopment of the fetus and according to research, the retardation of growth is not reversible. Also attributable to this syndrome are subnormal intelligence and lagging motor development. The syndrome results from poor physical condition of the alcoholic mother, plus the fact that alcohol ingested by the mother enters the blood system of the fetus. Children of alcoholic mothers often bear their children prematurely. These children are usually of low birth weight and suffer from a high rate of infant mortality. A problem foremost in alcoholics is vitamin deficiency. In the case of alcoholic mothers, this problem is compounded due to the vital role of vitamins in nourishment of the fetus.

The use of any drugs, particularly during the first three months of pregnancy, is dangerous. Most drug users are multiple drug users; they not only take the drug of their choice, but may also smoke and use other drugs to relieve all sorts of physical discomfort. The alcohol syndrome coupled with the use of other drugs can damage the fetus and also reduce the chances for later normal physical development of the child.

Physical development of the fetus can also be impaired when the father is the alcoholic partner. Effects of

anxiety and stress on expectant mothers have been established by research. Constant worrying about present conditions and fear of future problems after the baby arrives can
drain heavily upon the psychological resources of a preg-
nant woman.

At this point in time, it is not known to what extent
alcoholism affects heredity or whether or not there is an
inherited tendency to become alcoholic. Although various
perspectives have been offered, no conclusive evidence has
been presented on either side.

Physical concerns are important throughout a child's
life. Later in this chapter, during discussions of stages of
development, the physical aspect will be more closely
examined. However, one physical consideration that can
occur at any time in the environment of a child is physical
child abuse. The relationship between alcoholism and child
abuse is high, as children often become victims of the conflict experienced by their parents. It is important to realize
that not only the alcoholic may be a child abuser; the nonalcoholic parent may be one as well. Thus, the effects of
stress and feelings of the forms of physical abuse can cause
mental, physical, and emotional damage to its victims.
(Solomon, 1973) The consequences of being physically
beaten or attacked, as well as the fear of these behaviors,
have implications for development far beyond the physical harm suffered. What is probably the most disturbing of

this situation is that approximately one-half of abused children who are returned by courts to their parents eventually die of further abuse or neglect. (Fontana, 1976)

EMOTIONAL ASPECTS

It goes without saying that emotional development is a prime factor in personality development; how a child develops emotionally will influence how the child sees and can handle the world. Regardless of how many normal emotions may be experienced during development, children of alcoholics will also experience the emotions of fear and anxiety at various times. These feelings are present in all people, but for these children normal emotional development may not be sufficient to overcome them.

Central to skill in handling negative emotions is presence of a sense of security in relationships with other people. For children, security is usually found in the family, but in alcoholic families it is not always present. Absence of security can often produce undesirable or destructive defense mechanisms in children of alcoholics.

Throughout their development children are consistently confronted with change. They must face the challenge of growth, plus necessity to maintain the security of the past. Children of alcoholics encounter enormous growth problems, but possess little security from the past to draw upon. In light of this, much of their childhood and perhaps adult emotional development will be characterized by powerful defense mechanisms. Among these are regression, repression, sublimation, projection, and reaction formations. (Papalia and Olds)

Regression

In times of an alcohol crisis, children may regress to an earlier level of emotional or behavioral development by attempting to go back to a previous state of security (assuming that one existed). When the crisis has past they will return to their normal level of emotional development. This type of defense mechanism can be extremely complicated if the child has no solid sense of previous security to draw on. Continued repetition of alcoholic crises serves to compound the complications.

Repression

Repression is closely associated with anxiety-producing situations. It results in children negating feelings that are normally freely expressed. Children of alcoholics frequently repress their feelings in order to prevent "rocking the boat." They may also repress actions; for example, when deciding not to invite friends to their home because of the fear of unintended consequences.

Sublimation

Sublimation involves directing feelings of discomfort or anxiety to acceptable activities. Attempts at sublimation by children of alcoholics tend to be seen as positive aspects by most adults. A child's becoming a "workaholic" in school could be based upon sublimation of undesirable home conditions.

Projection

Projection means denial of unacceptable behaviors or situations by attributing them to others. Thus a child in an alcoholic home might ignore his or her own inappropriate behavior while (unrealistically) blaming another for the same behavior. The mechanism here functions to allow the child to disassociate from realities he or she cannot bear to face.

Reaction Formation

.Reaction formation is characterized by expression of the opposite of one's true feelings. The adolescent whose situation is known by his or her peers may consistently make jokes and light-hearted remarks about his or her home situation, when in reality the child is totally frustrated.

These above methods of coping with stress are all found in the emotional development of most children of alcoholics. Aside from the normal emotions associated with "growing" pains, children of alcoholics must handle a variety of emotions for which they may be ill equipped to handle due to an inadequate state of emotional development.

As emotional development continues, the child takes on a sense of identity or self-concept. Much of this self-concept is derived from the child's measuring his adequacy as defined by others. (Oswald, 1976) With the constant use of defense mechanisms, a true self-concept may never emerge. Some children of alcoholics feel that they were and are unwanted. They see themselves in positions of inferiority, inadequacy, and even worthlessness. Although such children behave in ways to generate the opinions others have of them, feedback they get from others serves to confirm their negative self-concepts.

PERSONALITY

Regardless of what theory is used to examine personality, all theories concur that much of one's personality is made up of life experiences. Many theorists of human development and personality divide life experiences into stages, each stage typified by different conflicts and crises which must be overcome in order to achieve adequate levels of development. It has also been postulated that each successive stage functions as building blocks for future stages. For many children of alcoholics the crises confronted in successive stages are compounded by unsolved problems left over from previous stages, plus the continuing stresses caused by living with an alcoholic parent. This compounding effect can have detrimental consequences for adequate personality development.

To illustrate these stages of compounded problems, the life stages of Erik Erikson are used under the next heading. (Erikson, 1963) Erikson's concepts were chosen because they are based more upon society's effect on a person rather than the person's effect on society. Children of alcoholics are often overwhelmed by their environment and have little chance to act upon it. At each stage of development Erikson sees particular conflicts that must be resolved in a positive manner. The success or failure of this resolution affect the handling of conflicts at future stages. As time passes, the child begins to establish a collection of positive and/or negative outcomes. If outcomes are mostly positive, the child will be better able to handle later adult roles.

(As mentioned earlier, not all children of alcoholic parents are affected in the same manner. Some will emerge from stages in their lives with a high ratio of positive conflict or crisis resolutions. Others will not.)

ALCOHOLISM
AND THE STAGES OF DEVELOPMENT

Trust Versus Mistrust

Erikson sees a sense of trust as the most vital element of a healthy personality. The formation of trust begins at birth and is crucial during the first year of life, when the infant is completely dependent on the fulfillment of basic needs. Maternal deprivation of an alcoholic mother can undermine the establishment of an infant's trust. The needs of the child may be ignored, attended as a last resort, or begrudgingly administered.

Even in cases where a baby's physical needs are satisfied, trust may not be established because of lack of emotional stability. The quantity of the relationship may not be as important as its quality. Whether the mother or father is alcoholic, the emotional drain on the parents may be so great that there is little emotional support left for the child to rely on. The seriousness of alcoholic parental role-inconsistency is gravely underestimated at this level because the child is nonverbal and helpless. Erikson feels that without a basic sense of trust in infancy the crises of later stages will be difficult to handle.

Not all children of alcoholics are born into alcoholic homes. Parental alcoholism may occur at later stages in their development. Those children who have established a sense of trust may be better able to handle the onset of alcoholism in a parent.

Autonomy Versus Shame and Doubt

A child must be able to achieve autonomy and yet accept the useful guidance of others. The contribution of parents during a child's growth is to administer reasonable and firm guidance when the quest for autonomy goes too far; a delicate balance between cooperation and willfulness is needed. In cases of excessive restrictions, autonomy is not achieved and is overshadowed by an emerging sense of shame in the child. A parent who wants to protect his or her child from the home environment may unwittingly limit childhood growth. The child is denied the opportunity to develop a sense of self-control because all forms of control, usually administered through restrictions, are supplied. The child may not be able to develop sufficient autonomy, resulting in a self-concept of inadequacy and shame.

Initiative Versus Guilt

Conflicts between initiative and guilt feelings begin in a four or five-year-old child, when his or her curiosity about the world is treated as inappropriate by adults. The child's questions are hushed up or ignored; sometimes even games and normal playful activities are stopped short or prohibited by parental commands that cause feelings of guilt in the child. In alcoholic homes such restrictions may be prevalent in the parent-child relationship because all family behavior is being dictated by the self-centeredness of the alcoholic.

Thus a balance between parental restrictiveness and permissiveness becomes desirable as the child grows; and consistency is the most important ingredient in this balance.

Erikson feels that inconsistency does more harm than being slightly too restrictive. Guilt emerges in the child when the responses to his or her behavior are unpredictable. In alcoholic homes inconsistency is a dominating factor. To overcome this the child may choose to over-conform, at the expense of subjugating initiative and creativity.

This stage is also characterized by observation and imitating of adult behavior. Role modeling, when performed by an alcoholic, can give a child inappropriate concepts of adult roles. The child sees alcoholism as an integral part of the role being played by either or both parents. It may not be until later years that some children realize that what they had observed was not normal adult behavior.

Industry Versus Inferiority

The typical child entering elementary school begins to develop a need to feel useful, commensurate with his or her growing ability to explore and achieve. This is what Erikson calls a "sense of industry." A crisis at this stage occurs if a sense of inadequacy or inferiority becomes dominant over the sense of industry. Although problems at this period are mostly concerned with school environment, a lack of parental interest in the child's accomplishments can compound the child's sense of inferiority, since the influence of parents on education during the elementary school years is particularly strong.

In the alcoholic home, feelings of uselessness can emerge in a child which will carry over into the school situation. A child who attempts varying behaviors or initiates actions that he or she hopes will be useful in alleviating problems at home, only to meet with failure at home, will tend to approach school feeling useless.

The elementary school child needs to feel that he or she is achieving goals, both educationally and socially; and parents of the elementary school child possess the key to providing him or her with a sense of accomplishment. Survival in school—the child's first step outside his or her primary environment—can depend upon the amount of self-esteem the child has developed within the home, plus the amount of support provided by parents when the child encounters school problems. Parents who show little interest in the child's school life may question poor performance in the upper grades and never realize their own contribution to the child's lack of success. Alcoholic parents may value education very highly, but because of drinking, guilt, and stress, be unable to provide the behavior necessary to help their child succeed in school.

Learning Identity Versus Identity Diffusion

The question "Who am I?" is closely related to development during adolescence. The crisis of this period evolves from normal attempts to establish a clear sense of identity. The adolescent is no longer identified as a child, but is not considered an adult.

Overidentification with negative characteristics is a problem that can occur at this stage. The adolescent sees himself or herself in terms of negative attitudes and rebellious actions. In alcoholic families such feelings are often already present, because the entire family feels deviant, making it more than normally difficult for the teenager to search for individual identity. A sense of personal identity is overshadowed by family identity.

If this identity stage has been entered with a previously-developed sense of inferiority, the crisis is intensified. Children who have been told that they are failures, inadequate, or have feelings of being unwanted are thus set up for later self-fulfilling prophecies.

Intimacy Versus Isolation

This stage is concerned with the ability to establish intimate relations with others. As previously mentioned, the ability to establish primary relations with others may be the single most important consideration for children of alcoholics.

When close relationships are unattainable, feelings of isolation arise. The young adult is hindered at a time when most people are sharing feelings and developing satisfying communication with others. An adolescent from an alcoholic home who is unable to achieve intimacy "has so much to live with and so little to live for." (Oswald, 1976) Such young adults may repress all inner feelings while displaying an outer pretense at being "normal." Such repression can result in loss of ability to become "card-carrying members of the human race."

Children who emerge emotionally affected from an alcoholic home may find themselves socially isolated. They have not had the opportunity to develop the life skills necessary to become fully functioning adults. They are forced to remain within themselves. The next stage of development is even more difficult.

Generativity Versus Self-Absorption

The effects of parental alcoholism do not disappear when offspring leave the home. Once patterns have been established they may continue throughout adulthood. Erikson assumes that the normal mature adult is capable of intimacy and possesses a strong identity. He feels that, in addition to these, the adult should have positive qualities to pass on to future generations. Some adults become parents, however, and have little to offer their children that could be called positive. They have been deprived of learning how to form interactions with others, so are paralyzed in relationships with their children. Unless such parents are able to overcome these problems, it is highly probable that the effects of being raised in an alcoholic family are passed along to at least one more generation. This becomes particularly frightening if children of alcoholics become alcoholic themselves and the process is continued.

Surviving an alcoholic home may take all a child has, so that in later life there is nothing left to give. The new adult is faced with psychological impoverishment. This becomes particularly frustrating to those who counted the days until they could leave the home environment, only to find that they do not possess the ability to improve their lives.

Integrity Versus Disgust

Erikson's last stage is development of integrity in the adult. A sense of integrity involves acceptance of responsibility for one's own life without blaming others for past or present misfortune. Unless children of alcoholics are able to achieve success at the previous life stages, this last stage appears to be impossible to attain.

When integrity is not developed, the individual finds it hard to accept life as it is. The person remains immaturely dependent on outside circumstances and makes statements such as, "I never could do what I want," or "If I had it to do over again, it would all be different."

ENVIRONMENTAL FEEDBACK

A final consideration for children who grow up in alcoholic homes is that they are influenced by their parents and consequently may develop similar personality characteristics. Although it is commonly agreed that there is no "alcoholic personality," it has been established that many alcoholics share certain personality characteristics such as anxiety, dependency, immaturity, inferiority, depression, and low self-esteem. (Forrest, 1975) If such characteristics are learned from role modeling, one can easily see that problems borne by children of alcoholics may be compounded when they reach adulthood. Many children of alcoholic parents become alcoholic themselves and the cyclical process continues to gain victims. This process seems assured, unless substitute environmental situations can attempt to counteract the disorganization and uncertainty of the home and family life. The potential source of positive actions to which we now turn is the school.

PART B

SUGGESTIONS FOR EDUCATORS

4

The Role of the School and the Teacher

Any school's program for children of alcoholic parents should be aimed specifically at the children themselves. The school should not become involved in the rehabilitation of alcoholic parents. On the surface, it may appear that working with the alcoholic parent is necessary. However, intervention involving treatment of parental alcoholism is outside the school's sphere of authority and probable competency.

Working with the children of alcoholics may appear to be an indirect approach; in some aspects this is true. But the school is not in the rehabilitation business. The school is in the education business, and direct involvement here means working directly with and in helping students. If through the school's efforts a change should occur in an alcoholic parent, this should be considered an incidental (albeit beneficial) side-effect.

AREAS OF SCHOOL CONCERN

A successful school program for children of alcoholic parents should be able to provide help by:

- Helping students to learn about alcohol and alcoholism.

- Helping teachers to deal with their own feelings toward alcohol use.

- Helping teachers to be perceived by their students as credible regarding alcohol use.

- Setting the right objectives for alcohol education.

- Developing a valid content for alcohol education.

- Involving students as active participants in alcohol education rather than as mere recipients of information.

- Helping children of alcoholics to express themselves—which many have difficulty doing.

- Helping children of alcoholics to gain an appropriate identity.

- Helping students to effectively relate to alcoholics and nonalcoholics.

- Referring children of alcoholics to other services when they can benefit from such assistance.

- Identifying children of alcoholic parents as part of an individualized educational program.

TEACHING ABOUT ALCOHOL

Aside from experiencing alcoholism's behavioral consquences, most children do not understand alcoholism or know what it is. Children from alcoholic homes tend to consider their circumstances unique and isolated. Education regarding the true facts about alcoholism clarifies the facts for such children. Myths must be exposed and disproved. Through various types of special classes, or by incorporating the subject into various existing classes, the school can provide information about alcohol and alcoholism (see appendix for suggested sources). A primary purpose of educational efforts in this area is to provide some relief through knowledge. Whether or not the home situation is solved, asking questions and obtaining true facts can provide some relief.

Since it is not possible to identify the children of alcoholics in all cases, comprehensive alcohol education should be provided in the classroom, where it should be treated as factually as any other subject. Under no circumstances should it be limited to education about living with an alcoholic parent. A realistic overview of the problem, presented from a neutral position, can supply a frame of reference which enables students to make responsible choices. The theme of responsible drinking, for those who will choose to drink, offers the framework to assess the use of alcohol in American society in a realistic manner. It is obvious that the majority of people in our society are not anti-alcohol, but are opposed to alcohol abuse and abusive behavior.

Educational classes can serve as vehicles to identify children of alcoholic parents since many of these children may, during or after class, ask questions that will indicate to the teacher an existing or potential problem at home. Using the theme of responsible drinking may help to reduce the high percentage of the children of alcoholics who become alcoholic themselves, and whose parental role models have consistently demonstrated irresponsible drinking.

Children who are shy or reluctant to ask questions will be best served if a good supply of free pamphlets are provided in a highly accessible area. There are many organizations that provide pamphlets on alcohol and alcoholism with topics ranging from drinking and driving to advice for children of alcoholics (see appendix). These pamphlets can usually be obtained free or at minimal cost. In many school libraries, books on alcoholism are often "missing" from the shelves. This indicates interest in the subject, but also indicates perceived embarrassment in checking the books out.

The Feelings of Teachers

In the early 1900's when alcohol education began to gain in popularity in America, the major theme in school was one of temperance in using alcohol. By the 1920's, however, this orientation of temperance shifted to reflect the prohibition movement. Abstinence was advocated. The effects of these themes in alcohol education of abstinence and temperance are difficult to evaluate. Certainly temperance or abstinence of alcohol use is not in itself harmful. However, the manner in which abstinence and temperance were pressed upon students may have produced a number of undesired results including beliefs about alcohol. Both the temperance and abstinence programs in schools through the 1920's contended that any amount of alcohol use was wrong and concentrated on the "disasterous" effects of drinking.

During the 1930's little was said about alcohol education. Perhaps this was in reaction to the repeal of prohibition. However, in the 1940's, the very negative aspects of alcohol use by adults (alcoholism, broken homes, and skid-row stories) were being emphasized in school programs. In the 1950's American schools broadened this concern to include teenage alcohol use while still stressing horror stories in teaching about alcohol. The evils of using alcohol became central material for courses.

During the 1960's alcohol education took a backseat to an emerging concern to stop the use among students of other drugs such as marijuana and amphetamines. The approach of drug education in the 1960's clearly followed the traditional mode. However, like the alcohol education programs, it was characterized by the scare tactics preceding it. The use of alcohol and other drugs by our youth was not impeded. In fact, during the early 1970's the use of alcohol by teenagers was almost applauded since it was considered a move away from the "drug scene." By the mid-seventies we were confronted with increasing reports of teenage alcoholism, and again approaches emphasizing the evils of drinking were stressed. In summary, alcohol education has remained in many schools what it was in the early 1900's.

One unfortunate result of seventy years of alcohol education tradition is that it has left present day educators with a "poor track record" in alcohol education and few guidelines for improvement. Teachers with responsibilities for alcohol education still face critical problems, and in facing them many are ill-prepared. Many lack confidence because they do not understand, in an objective way, the functions of alcohol.

Initially, teachers must examine their own attitudes about alcohol and their own drinking habits. If negativism is to be overcome in alcohol education, it must be replaced by objectivity. Our biases for or against alcohol will make this difficult. Many of our biased attitudes stem from personal drinking habits or our contact with those who drink. This contact can be responsible for biased positive or negative attitudes. One who has had unfortunate experiences because of the alcohol use of others and has not worked them out can be just as detrimental to desired educational endeavors as one whose own drinking habits are questionable. We cannot be so naive to assume that educators are immune to alcohol problems.

TEACHER CREDIBILITY

The subject of teacher credibility, regardless of subject taught, is an important consideration in effective teaching. Nowhere, however, has credibility in the classroom been challenged more than by those receiving alcohol and other drug education. Teacher credibility in these areas has suffered because of the lack of objectivity and a failure to be concerned with previous attempts to educate students regarding substance abuse. Much of credibility has to do with the relationship between the message given and the message received. Will students perceive the teacher as knowledgeable on these subjects? How will teachers handle the questions of "Do you drink?" or "Have you ever had too much to drink?" "What is too much?"

Credibility in alcohol education can be lost because of perceived personal bias in presentation. If one of the goals of alcohol education is to help students make their own choices, we should not be viewed as dictating preferences for them. Even if appropriate preferences are advocated, they may be seen as not realistic if the teacher is viewed as one who does not understand "today's world."

The issues of teacher credibility in alcohol education are similar to teacher credibility problems in other areas. The establishment of credibility is dependent upon many factors ranging from influence and power to knowledge and attractiveness. However, factual data presented in an objective manner which encourages honest responses from students will greatly enhance the teachers' credibility in alcohol education.

OBJECTIVES FOR ALCOHOL EDUCATION

As a prelude to gaining credibility, it will be helpful if the teachers of alcohol education become clear about what alcohol education includes and does not include, including objectives, content, and procedures. What is alcohol education? Does it consist of the effects of alcohol in the body, problems of alcoholism, how to live with an alcoholic, or guidelines on drinking and driving?

A severe problem of past alcohol education has been the almost universal lack of a clear definition of alcohol education. At the classroom level there is a need to decide upon what is alcohol education. Too often to fulfill a state requirement, a teacher is called upon to teach an alcohol education class or unit. "What do I teach?" is asked. "Oh, whatever you like; we need to complete ten hours of instruction" is mumbled in reply. What is needed is a clear statement of intent or teaching objectives that are attainable within the time frame of the course.

THE CONTENT OF ALCOHOL EDUCATION

Closely associated with the past lack in specifying the teaching objectives of alcohol education is the inconsistency of much of the course contents of a typical program.

For example, another problem concerns the appropriateness of the material for the given students. Alcohol education in the fifth grade should not be the same as in the senior year of high school. The needs of the students are different. In elementary school, although research indicates that the majority of students have already tried alcohol, their interests lie in what alcohol is and why people drink it. Students in the middle school years want to know specific details about alcohol, such as the different types of drinks, what happens to the body after using alcohol, how much is safe, and again why use alcohol. Senior high students' concerns are more directly related to the use of alcohol and behavioral consequences. Interest ranges from drinking and driving to health and personal problems associated with consumption. Another topic often discussed is the relationship to or comparison of alcohol with other drugs. Can you mix alcohol with other drugs? And the classic question of alcohol versus marijuana. In other words, as students get older, their experiences with alcohol and their needs for information become more personal.

A course in alcohol education should be structured similar to the way other school subjects are taught throughout the educational process, i.e., history, science, etc. Most courses are taught on a building block assumption according to perceived levels of understanding and the difficulty of the material. The extensiveness of American history courses in elementary school are different from that of high school, yet it is the same topic. Alcohol education should be handled in a similar fashion.

Another important curriculum decision is: Should alcohol education be incorporated in existing classes or in separate classes? If so, where? Is it a health concern, a chemical discussion for science, a social problem, or an analysis of free enterprise for business courses? These concerns must be handled by school districts prior to alcohol education attempts. Much of the inconsistency can be avoided by timely discussions and a more universal approach.

A similar concern that needs to be considered is the priority that the subject of alcohol receives wherever it is taught. Usually alcohol education receives rather low priority. This low priority is reflected in the lack of support, minimal, if any, course guidance, and a philosophy of the course as a necessary evil to fulfill requirements.

Low priority is also reflected by the manner in which some teachers are "drafted" to teach the subject. Simply having the course taught becomes more important than who teaches it. This overrides the idea that the teacher may be the single most important factor in alcohol education. The school systems will need to decide if they actually value alcohol education or merely value saying that they do. Lack of information and resources and in-service training will hinder the teacher of alcohol education.

CHILDREN NEED TO TALK

The aim of verbalization is to provide opportunities for children to express and ventilate their feelings about their alcoholic parents, their nonalcoholic parents, and alcoholism in general. It is an opportunity to release pent up shame, guilt, fears, and confusion in order to arrive at an impression of parental alcoholism's effect on the individual child.

Getting a child to verbalize may not be easy. It cannot be assumed that the child will want to talk—particularly one whose faith in adults may have been inhibited by painful past experiences with adults. Verbal communication is often tentative for the children of the alcoholic (Hecht, 1977) because children of alcoholics often rely heavily on environmental feedback for a sense of being. Positive environmental feedback can be supplied by the school, but a teacher must realize that in addition to lacking trust in adults, such children may be totally devoid of positive attitudes towards anyone in a position of authority. Feelings of estrangement and powerlessness govern the child who is in an alienated state.

Adding to the difficulty of verbalizing is the fact that such children generally consider discussion of the home situation as "taboo." They may have been ordered by a nonalcoholic parent not to discuss the matter with anyone.

They may have been told that nothing is wrong, but perceive that something is, but do not know how to define it. Also, teachers must understand that children may be ashamed and embarrassed to discuss their home situation. Consequently, the teacher's approach should be matter-of-fact and friendly, but not overly-sympathetic; for above all, these children seldom want pity.

Once a teacher gains the confidence of the child and verbalization occurs, the rewards can be enormous. The greatest benefit (and the primary benefit of verbalization) may not be derived from the solving of anything, but merely from "letting the dam burst." Satisfaction and relief can be gained from just sharing or releasing emotions.

At this point, the teacher must remember that his or her role is best served by concentrating on and staying with the feelings of the child. This is not the time to talk about dealing with the alcoholic parent. Nor should judgement be passed on what the child reveals. Such a child has experienced enough negative aspects of the situation, and a great deal of positive or neutral acceptance is needed. In early dialogue with a teacher, the student is apt to be confused about his or her situation and will appreciate encouragement in finding words to share long-inhibited feelings and confidences.

But identifying these children and revealing their problems is just the beginning. With tact and empathy, a skillful teacher can do much to help the child gain a positive self-concept. Gaining trust and confidence will not only open the "family secret," but will also make available to the child an important source of security—a responsible, interested adult.

THE STUDENT'S IDENTITY

Children of alcoholics need to be able to see themselves apart from alcoholism. Assisting them in realizing that they are entitled to lives of their own (self-realization) can be part of the school's function. Schools offer many opportunities for children to achieve self-realization, as well as concerned adults who are able to convey a sense of self-realization to children.

Self-realization is closely associated with the idea of self-concept—amount of belief in one's own abilities. It is not necessary to elaborate upon the relationship between self-concept and academic achievement; one has only to read hundreds of articles and research findings. Obviously, developing a positive self-concept can facilitate a child's achieving self-realization. Often a child may be so absorbed in his or her family situation that he or she develops little or no self-realization, because individual family roles and achievements have been overshadowed by the presence of alcoholism. It becomes important for the teacher to steer discussion away from home problems and to center it on the children and their feelings. The teacher should emphasize that children's feelings are not only important, but natural. A teacher can—and should—convey to children that it is acceptable for them to be concerned about themselves.

The child need not be an extension of the alcoholic. The school is a community and the student is a citizen of that community. Feeling a part of the community can do much to enhance a child's perception that he or she has a role other than living with an alcoholic.

THE RELATIONSHIPS OF STUDENTS

The most important opportunity that the school can provide for children of alcoholic parents is that of developing positive primary relationships. Some children of alcoholics will already have strong primary relationships. These have been designated in the "have" category and they tend to function fairly well, due to the fact that the impact of alcoholism on their lives is being somewhat neutralized by their relationships with others. Many "haves" are extremely self-sufficient, possess a high degree of self-discipline, receive high demands on performance from their parents, or feel that approved academic and/or social performance will give them a position of family status. With the internalization of these attributes plus the support of primary relationships, they may be better equipped to meet the challenges of the school than children from nonalcoholic families. These children, who have the most going for them will successfully survive both the home situation and school.

Children that the school can benefit most are those who do not possess primary relationships. In school, opportunities for interaction with others is greatest and an aware teacher can encourage maximum involvement. Most schools have extensive extracurricular activities which can provide the foundations for a high degree of personal contact, and at the same time help students to achieve self-realization. Some children need only encouragement to join a club, try out for a team, or volunteer their services. Other children may be reluctant, since they see membership in any organization as an added responsibility and feel that the responsibility of their home life is enough. In these instances, the teacher may not want to recommend maximum involvement at the outset. It might be better to start with involvement that is partial or of short duration, such as a seasonal activity. Exposure to others is the desired initial effect, and the student may make a decision later to accept added activities.

For some students, teachers themselves represent a primary relationship. In this role, the teacher must be alert to value judgements. It is necessary to maintain a teacher-student relationship and not internalize the situation of the student. The role of the teacher should be one of "detached warmth." The teacher's attitudes convey: "I want to help, I will assist you, I can refer you, but I cannot do it for you." The teacher becomes the guide to a path of self-realization, not the creator of it.

REFERRALS

The final area of service for the school and the teacher is to become a source of referral. No teacher can teach all things to all students. If a program is to be successful, it is essential to know what resources are available for the assistance of children of alcoholics. Alcohol Information Services are available in most communities. For areas lacking local services, a list of national organizations is furnished in the appendix of this book.

Contacting and using local services will be discussed in Chapter Five, *The Administrators.* Referrals should not be limited, however, to agencies specializing in alcoholism. Some referrals may be made within the school itself—such as advice that the child join a certain club or seek information from another teacher. Students may relate to some teachers better than to others. The teacher who first learns of a student's problems may not be the one the student prefers for communication or assistance.

Knowing the resources in one thing, using them is another. Most local agencies are willing to come to a school and offer assistance or information; but they seldom do so unless made aware that their services are needed. A guest speaker whose talk is followed by an informal question and answer session is one beneficial service provided free of charge by most agencies concerned with alcohol education.

IDENTIFYING
CHILDREN OF ALCOHOLIC PARENTS

There are no specific criteria for easy identification of children whose parents are alcoholics. In fact, many of the behaviors of such children are similar to those stemming from other kinds of family problems or situations. The teacher must be able to observe symptomatic behavior patterns and rely on intuition. These patterns will be what will help to distinguish between children of alcoholic parents and other types of problems manifested by children. Aggressive behavior and "acting out" constitute only one behavior pattern that should be noticed. Although some children of alcoholics will indeed act out, others may exhibit patterns of withdrawal or defensiveness.

It is important to remember that individual or single behavioral acts do not constitute behavioral patterns. The teacher must be careful not be jump to conclusions or label children too quickly. The important aspect in identifying these children is the development of patterns, which may either appear in an obvious fashion or require astute observation to discern them. Some behavior patterns which might indicate alcoholism in the student's home are described in the following paragraphs.

Appearance

The overall appearance of a child may reflect his or her home situation. As the home environment fluctuates, so does the child's appearance. The patterns of appearance may reflect the drinking patterns of the alcoholic parent.

If a young child comes to school in an overall untidy condition (dirty clothes, torn apparel, or lacking in personal hygiene), parental indifference or neglect are suggested. This may show itself in a pattern if the child's dress and appearance change from one day to another. If Mondays are particularly "sloppy" days, perhaps the weekend home environment is less than adequate.

Also, the physical condition of the child may indicate physical abuse in the home. The relationship between alcoholic parents and child abuse is unfortunately high. Physical education teachers, school health personnel, coaches, and any other school employee who consistently notices bruises on a child should report it to an administrator. Children who are consistently or frequently bruised should be watched carefully. Also, children who frequently offer excuses so as not to partake in physical education may be doing so in order to avoid the exposure of a physical condition.

Academic Performance

Sporadic variation in academic performance is a key indicator of sporadic variation in a child's home circumstances. A student may perform well when the home situation is calm and do poorly when the home situation is in shambles. Fluctuating academic performance is noticeable to an alert teacher who begins to see regular patterns in the student's periods of achievement and nonachievement, apparently without noticeable reason. Sometimes children from alcoholic homes exhibit better academic performance on certain days of the week, or during certain times of the month. In some, such a pattern may even show itself during certain times of each day. Many children who are concerned about going home may perform well all day and then do poorly or lose attentiveness during the last class of the day.

Report Cards

Parental report card signatures may develop a certain pattern. A familiar pattern for children of alcoholics may be that one parent signs the report card on the occasions it is returned on time, and that the other parent signs the card when it is returned late. Although this may be a minor point, it can serve as a clue when other patterns are present that might suggest alcoholism. The nonalcoholic parent may sign the report card whether both parents have seen it or not. However, if the alcoholic parent was too inebriated to look at or understand the report card, the nonalcoholic may decide to wait for him or her to see it. Since this waiting period may mean returning it late, the alcoholic will usually be asked to sign it since it was he or she who caused the waiting.

Whenever a report card reflects drastic change in a student's performance, either positive or negative, the teacher might ask the child how it was received at home and get a reply to the effect that it was little noticed. This reply, if accompanied by negative "body language," indicates disappointment in parental concern and may be indicative of severe home problems.

Peers

Since some children of alcoholics will already have good primary relationships with others, those without friends may be the most noticeable. Children who are too silent in class, walk by themselves in the hallways, and are otherwise constant "loners" demonstrate symptoms of social disengagement. Also, a child may have only one or two friends who inadvertently mention such things as, "Carol is sad because things are not too good at home." Such clues should be considered by her teachers.

In some situations children of alcoholics are ostracized and avoided by other children. Sometimes (in cases where a parent has engaged in public drunkenness) children are made the brunt of ignorant jokes. Also, some children from "normal" homes may be warned by their parents against associating with them; others may repeat gossip overheard at home. It is little wonder under such conditions that many children from alcoholic homes often voluntarily avoid contact with other children. They are loners by force, not by choice.

At the other extreme are children of alcoholics who, like other children, try to compensate for being ignored at home by demanding excessive attention in school. Such children may be said to be "acting out." The attention these children get from teachers usually consists of various types of punishment. However, teachers should be alert to recognize possible underlying environmental causes of attention seeking behavior. Being the "class clown" may be one method of trying to establish valued relationships with peers when one is starved for attention at home. A poor academic performer may find that by entertaining others, he or she attains some value to others in being at school. It becomes easier for such a person to stay in school. It is their way of coping with a poor school situation.

The various types of coping behaviors mentioned here are not significant when they occur infrequently or individually, but they often contribute to particular difficulties for children of alcoholics. Therefore it is of considerable importance that students whose parents are alcoholics be identified for help. The next step is to gain the trust and confidence of these students.

In the case of children of alcoholic parents, gaining their trust can be an especially difficult task, since they may have few bonds with adults, even fewer with teachers, and in fact may regard the entire school situation to be devoid of any significant bonds. The school may enter their lives, but be viewed with resignation or cynicism and hostility, even if not overly expressed. Students who view school as a poor place to be and must add this to their problems at home, experience considerable frustration. The source of this frustration may be particularly difficult to ascertain by the student. The student may blame their academic inadequacies or the school.

On the other hand, the student who leads a turbulent home life may find the school as a place of rest, a place where he or she is able to maintain a low profile and escape the traumas of family living. The school for many children of alcoholics can be the place for rest from home life with little in the way of desired learning taking place. For other students of alcoholics, school may be the place where considerable personal, social, and intellectual attainments occur while being rested from the fatigue acquired at home. In other words, school can be more than a sanctuary for children of alcoholics—it can be a place where they are helped. This is especially true if the students whose parents are alcoholic are recognized.

Therefore, educators should be alert to the behavioral symptoms common in children of alcoholics. After students whose parents are alcoholics are recognized, the school can more effectively utilize its resources in order to achieve for these children growth in attitudes, values, skills, and knowledge.

Read° Read Read Read⁶ Read

. NOTE .

I told my mom about you speakers
I told her about the things
it could do My Mom is
an Alcoholic I convinced her
into going to the State Hospital
she is going I THANK YOU

VERY MUCH FOR COMING
TO OUR SCHOOl.

Read

One of several letters written to the author by a student in the eighth
grade class at Watson Junior High School, Colorado Springs, Colorado.

5

The Administrators

A deservable program that meets the needs of students with alcoholic parents will be mutually supported by school administrators and their staffs. They will work together. The entire staff will be able to recognize and be sensitive to the symptoms and problems of coming from an alcoholic home. The staff will also be familiar with resources that are available to them for achieving their objective of helping children of alcoholics. Of course, the accomplishment of any successful school objective depends to a considerable extent on the supervisory roles of administrators as they work to mutually involve teachers and other staff in the planning and implementation of activities.

Until recently, many administrators have hesitated to get involved in focusing on children of alcoholics, asking, "Is this an issue that really concerns the school?" Obviously, the family problems of all children have educational implications; children of alcoholics are no different than others in this regard.

Furthermore, the school's role is to work with students and not to work with the alcoholic problems of the parents of students. However, the school should work with students who have alcoholic parents so that they may develop the same kinds of personal and social strengths that are advocated for all students.

It is possible that some will feel a need to question the legality of taking into account family conditions such as alcoholism when planning educational programs. On the other hand, since the overall purpose of a sound program to help children of alcoholics is to help them attain the same goals as are held for all students, and neither the students nor their parents will be subjected to an inquisition regarding drinking habits, it is doubtful that legal difficulties will emerge. However, should educators find themselves heading toward legal problems, the nature of their involvement with parents and students should be quickly reassessed.

Even if there are no legal problems, the question of taking into account alcoholic conditions in the family may, nonetheless, bring up ethical or moral concerns. The position may be taken by some that alcoholic parents are strictly a family problem, and that any problems which result at school because of home conditions are entirely a family matter; the family is the only one responsible. However, we know that the school and family are not that separate in their influence; actually they greatly affect each other. Furthermore, many attempts are constantly going on to ameliorate poor conditions at home. Many lunch programs and other compensatory education programs have been developed to help children overcome the difficulties of background. The same kinds of needs are there for others. In fact, by federal and state law, the schools are now concerned about child abuse and neglect at home.

However, if the schools are going to efficiently take into account the rather unique problems of students, including those whose parents are alcoholic, then the leadership of school administrators becomes crucial. There are four areas, among others, that the leadership skills of administrators should initially focus upon. They are: 1) in-service training, 2) development of resources, 3) policy support, and 4) program coordination. Effective educational leadership in these four areas can become the catalyst for development and maintenance of a successful program.

IN-SERVICE TRAINING

The area of staff in-service training is a vital function for all schools, since at these sessions up-to-date techniques and issues can be brought forth. In an effective program for students with alcoholic parents, in-service training should fulfill several goals.

One objective of in-service training should be to sensitize school staff to the presence of students with special problems stemming from alcoholic conditions at home. The staff needs to become aware of what alcoholism is and is not and its impact on families. A second objective should be to deal with questions about what teachers and other school staff should and should not do in working with children of alcoholics. A third aim of in-service programs should be to provide alcohol education materials and suggestions for what the school staff can do in a variety of situations at school. Topics to explore during in-service training should cover various methods for getting students to be more aware of their own potential, to be able to better express their feelings, and to be more clear about their values. There are many communication techniques and exercises in the areas of value clarification and group dynamics which can facilitate discussion and provide vehicles to self-expression and self-awareness for children of alcoholics, as well as others.

In-service training need not be limited to the subjects of alcohol, alcoholism, or the children of alcoholic parents. It is not necessary to dwell upon the topic of alcohol. The real benefits of in-service training will be derived from developing some practical guidelines for the school for its own philosophy and procedural arrangements to meet the needs of its children from alcoholic homes.

In-service training on the subject of children of alcoholic parents must be followed up. Assuming that the first few sessions have been able to sensitize personnel, it becomes imperative that sessions be arranged for discussions and guidelines after real situations have been encountered. Asking teachers or other school personnel to become aware of a situation without providing avenues of feedback and growth is often self-defeating; it may in fact increase levels of teacher frustration of inadequacy, since recognition of a problem can become very taxing if the means to solve it are not made available.

DEVELOPMENT OF RESOURCES

Most communities fall under a county or state program for substance abuse which is normally affiliated with the county or state health department. These programs can help with in-service training, loan or recommendation of films and publications, and the providing of guest speakers. Administrators may want to seek advice from a substance abuse agency to explore ideas and alternative methods. Some communities have several programs working in the area of alcohol and drug rehabilitation, all of which are eager to furnish assistance in setting up and maintaining school services to children of alcoholics.

Many programs and agencies at the national level can also provide access to excellent resource materials. Time and effort in finding materials can be reduced by corresponding with national agencies, specifying the type of program, and asking for assistance and materials. However, face-to-face contact with local persons, rather than national speakers, should be utilized whenever possible in order to fit the individual needs of the school.

At the national level is an organization called Alateen. This is a group solidarity-based organization operating very similarly to Al-Anon, which is an organization for the non-alcoholic spouses of alcoholics. Members of Alateen are children of alcoholic parents, and the basic purpose of Alateen is to help such children appreciate or understand their identities. It also explores the plight of the alcoholic and possible ways of helping or at least coping with an alcoholic parent. The benefits of this organization can be considerable since children in each group are able, in settings of confidentiality, to share a problem they all have in common. A better understanding of parents, a better self-concept, and increased self-confidence usually result. By corresponding with the national Alateen organization, one can obtain information about Alateen meetings in their areas, or get advice on how to ask the local Al-Anon chapter to start one of these groups for youngsters in your area.

Although Alateen is not formally affiliated with or sponsored by any specific organization, it utilizes various public facilities for meetings. The school building could be an excellent place to start a new chapter, however, it should *not* be officially sponsored by the school.

Another resource for all kinds of help that may be effectively utilized is Alcoholics Anonymous. Although anonymity is a characteristic of the organization, there are many recovering alcoholics who are willing to speak openly on the subject. Many recovering alcoholics are parents themselves and would welcome the opportunity to become involved in a school program. This can usually be arranged through the local resources or a call to the local AA chapter. In many communities, AA membership and its power are seldom comprehended by the general public. AA is one of the best resources available to a school: a "people" resource rich in experience.

Additional community resources that are often found beneficial are social organizations and agencies working with family problems, child abuse, child guidance, and self-help of various kinds. Many communities contain a college or university that offers courses in family and substance abuse, from which a willing instructor might be utilized for in-service training.

There are many resources available at the local, state, federal, and national level which can be helpful in developing programs for children of alcoholics. The appendix contains agency addresses and suggested resources that can be beneficial to a school program for children of alcoholics.

The key to successful resource utilization is to take advantage of every available means.

POLICY SUPPORT

Any program to assist children of alcoholic parents needs to be supported if it is to be successful; and, like in-service training, support must be followed up to be successful. Follow-up will allow for the ironing out of initial policy problems and helps to shape the eventual direction of the program.

A school's policy on a program of this nature can be formal or informal. Specific guidelines and policy statements will be utilized in a formal program, whereas informal programs will operate in a less structured manner. The amount of formalization will depend partially upon prevailing attitudes in a district. Attitudes are generally influenced by the community's tolerance of the use of alcohol, and certainly the drinking patterns of those making the decisions will have an impact.

In the development of school policy, the role of the school is supporting children—while avoiding direct involvement in the problems of their alcoholic parents—and must be completely understood by everyone. It should also be clear that such a program is not the same as alcohol education—even though alcohol education may be in the curriculum, and used as an aid in identifying children of alcoholics. A program to help the children of alcoholic parents is not a matter of curriculum development alone. It is a question of using the positive aspects of the community and school atmosphere to assist in the growth of children who need support and guidance outside their home environment.

Another aspect of policy support is monetary. In-service training, guest speakers, and the purchase of reference materials will take some money and time of staff; however, it is doubtful that such costs will be excessive. Materials can be obtained from various agencies at little or no cost. Nevertheless, it is usually necessary to have some monetary arrangements initiated by the school administrator for incidental expenses such as film rental or acquisition of special materials.

PROGRAM COORDINATION

Critical to the overall success of a program for children of alcoholics will be the coordination of the various aspects of the program. This will involve not only the managing of the program within the school, but also within the community.

At the school level, decisions will need to be made regarding how the program will operate, who is involved, and their level of involvement. Admistrators may want to coordinate these activities themselves or delegate an individual or group for these responsibilities. Programs will achieve more success if a single source of information is available, such as a resource room for information material, knowing who is in charge of what phase, and the role or roles of school personnel in the program. Knowing who to go to will enhance cooperation and involvement by school personnel.

Coordination outside of school will include establishing rapport with local resource personnel and building community support for the program. Also, existing community programs for students will provide additional alternatives for working with children of alcoholics. These programs could include other types of self-help groups, as well as opportunities for recreational group membership.

The goal of coordination will be to keep sections of the school program from becoming fragmented or isolated. Substantial interaction within as well as outside of the program is necessary for success. Not only will this enhance program effectiveness, but it will also provide avenues of feedback regarding the strong and weak aspects of the program.

SUMMARY

The mutual support of all school personnel is a must if a program to help students of alcoholic parents is to have a chance at success. The responsibility for this support will belong to all school employees, but it will be much easier for a program to succeed if it is actively endorsed by school administrators.

Raising the level of awareness of the plight of students from alcoholic homes will not be enough. Guidelines for help, establishment of resources, and involvement with these students is necessary. All of these endeavors will require support and coordination.

6

Outside of the Classroom

All educators can help children of alcoholics. Regardless of whether you are a teacher, school nurse, counselor, social worker, librarian, club advisor, or director of a school activity, you will have many opportunities to help students with home problems. If you take advantage of your opportunities, there are at least three things you can do to help those who have a parent who is an alcoholic.

The first thing that you can do is to be an effective listener and communicator. This means that you should help your students to be able to express their feelings and thereby deal with their fears and aspirations. One of the more unfortunate problems experienced by some children of alcoholics is that they have no one to talk with about their needs, fears, and hopes.

A second thing that you can do for students of alcoholics is to facilitate their skills in developing needed primary relationships with other students and adults. Some children of alcoholics have a difficult time in relating to their peers and adults. Like all students, they need opportunities to participate with others in primary group activities. However, many children of alcoholics need supportive counseling to be effective in using group activities to foster needed primary group relationships.

The third opportunity that you should not miss when it avails itself is to carefully observe your students and their situations. What you observe can be essential to being of assistance to them. Counselors, school nurses and coaches often have a special advantage in being able to observe conditions about which the student, their families, or other professionals very much need to know.

LISTENING AND COMMUNICATING

Counselors and school social workers typically have responsibilities for listening, advising, counseling, and sometimes providing therapy to students. In part, others also share these roles. While it is not a formal requirement that coaches and club advisors act as counselors, they may act in ways consonant with good counseling. Within certain restrictions, every educator should help students to talk about what they like and dislike about their lives. However, it is important to know when assistance from other professionals is necessary. In this regard, each educator needs to have knowledge of his or her own competencies and limitations.

Know Your Limitations

Of course, all professional staff will need to consider their legal, ethical and professional obligations as well as their competencies in deciding what they should and should not do with students. It is very important that educators seek assistance in areas where they are not authorized to function. If they are not trained as therapists, they should not try and act as therapists. If there is any doubt about the severity of a student's personal or social problems, there are usually counselors, school psychologists or school social workers available who will gladly offer their assistance.

When Talking with Students

Of course, the need for you does not cease after a student reveals to you that he or she has an alcoholic parent. Rather, the need for effective educators is intensified. It is often after confiding about one's problem that the benefits of interacting with others occurs most.

A viable concern at this point may be how the parents will react to their child's confiding in someone outside the family. Will an irate alcoholic parent come to school complaining that you have interfered in their family's private business? However, if you limit your discussions with students to the student's feelings and to an understanding of what alcoholism is, there probably will be no cause for parent concern. Furthermore, if care is taken to avoid communicating that the student's difficulties are those of his or her parent's alcoholism and you direct attention to the student's school and social performance, the parent is very likely to welcome your help.

As a sidelight, the expression of denial of any drinking related problems is deemed important by those alcoholic parents who want to continue drinking. Similarly, the spouse of an alcoholic may have his or her felt need to refrain from talking about drinking related difficulties. Consequently, in parent contacts it is probable that alcoholism will not be a matter for discussion. And if the topic comes up, perhaps you should remain silent on the subject of the parent's drinking.

In the exploration of peer relationships with either the parents or their children, there are several factors to consider. The benefits of getting students involved in extra-curricular activities have already been mentioned. Another suggestion is to foster situations whereby certain children of alcoholic parents can become involved with one another. Since one of the problems in working with students who have an alcoholic parent is inducing them to "open up," it may be easier for them to talk with their peers who have similar experiences than it is for them to confide in an adult.

Group activities and discussions can be especially effective with teenagers since they are in an age bracket where they are adopting new values. One value that is fostered in youth groups appears to be a concern for each others' welfare. It may be a good idea to have the students consider calling each other at home when times are bad. They can use the mutual support of their peers in maintaining their poise and compassion.

If a student discussion group is formed, it should not be identified as being focused upon alcohol problems. Moreover, since there are many types of family problems affecting educational outcomes, such a group may take on any number of organizational themes and objectives. Such themes as "understanding your parents better" may be employed. A general approach would also reduce any embarrassment at being involved in an activity that is known for dealing with certain home problems. Also, since the primary purpose of a group discussion should be to meet student's needs, an organizational theme dealing with "self-awareness" and examining personal feelings may be appropriate.

If group discussion appears to be too formal or stigmatizing, a "walk-in center" for students may prove workable. A walk-in center can serve as a multiple program for students meeting various needs by dealing not only with home life, but with their many other problems. Such a center would be an obvious place for not only activities and discussions, but also as a place where they can obtain information on a variety of subjects ranging from alcohol and drug use to whatever else concerns them.

Remember, whatever the activity that is fostered, at all times it must be clear that the purpose of group discussions and walk-in centers should be to assist students; they should not attempt changes in the student's home environment.

In attempting to establish group interactions, it should also be borne in mind that many children of alcoholics find it difficult to make new friends. Many are very withdrawn or complete loners. The professional educator may be aware of the benefits to be derived from peer relationships, but their skills will be put to a test to prove such benefits to a student who has never had friends. They must also be prepared to be helpful when something goes wrong, after a student takes advice to seek friendship. Perhaps the student has confided in someone who did not understand, or worse yet, subjected the student to ridicule.

Perhaps your greatest contribution will be in the areas of helping students to discover that their feelings are normal and that it is normal to be confused and sometimes upset about one's home environment. Exploring a student's feelings with him or her can help you to obtain a better understanding of that student. More importantly, an exploring of feelings may allow the student to grow in self-understanding.

FACILITATING PRIMARY RELATIONSHIPS

School personnel who lead extracurricular activities have many opportunities to assist in the establishment of primary relationships for students who are children of alcoholic parents. Like others, these students can acquire many benefits from extracurricular activities. However, for children of alcoholics, the more obvious benefits of extracurricular activities may be secondary to the benefits achieved through establishment and maintenance of peer relationships. The student not only learns how to take part in a sport, publish a newspaper, etc., but also gains a sense of belonging and a role that he or she values.

A vital role that you can have in the case of children of alcoholic parents is in getting them invovled. However, recruiting children of alcoholics into group activities may be more difficult than directing them once they join. This is true because many such students are not eager to join school groups. This is particularly true if they feel that an extracurricular activity is just another responsibility to endure, rather than a vehicle by which they can reduce the strain of existing responsibilities. Furthermore, when a student's feelings of self-worth are minimal, he or she may feel incapable of contributing anything to a group and may have to be persuaded that his or her participation is needed.

Nonclassroom activities can also serve to reduce the time spent by children of alcoholic parents in uncomfortable situations. This is very desirable in itself. More importantly, however, extracurricular activities provide more time and opportunities for such children to interact with you and other potential adult role models. In addition, some students may feel that an educator outside of the classroom is more approachable than a teacher within a classroom, or that it is more permissible to discuss "after school" matters after school.

MAKING OBSERVATIONS

When you are with students, of course, you need to be very observant if you are to help them in achieving an understanding of their conditions. Your observations may focus on their peer relationships, academic interests, achievements, reasons for talking to you about their problems, willingness to share attitudes and confidences, and their evaluations of their home situation. This last concern will probably be difficult for you to explore and may depend more in the beginning on how they act than on what they say.

When you are near students, there are a number of things about which you should be sensitive. Among these are physically observable symptoms which may reflect serious home problems, such as chronic fatigue, confusion, or emotional strain. Although all educators should be sensitive to these symptoms, health care professionals can play an especially vital role in making valid observations of students who are suspected of having health related problems which stem from their home life.

Because of their focused interest and training in health, nurses and physical activity directors can detect subtle details of a student's appearance beyond those of obvious bruises that might suggest parental abuse or neglect. Bruises concealed by clothing can come under their scrutiny. Also, students suffering symptoms of strain are usually more noticeable to health workers than others. Health workers are also aware of students who have frequent headaches, high levels of anxiety, and constant fatigue.

However, if child abuse or neglect is suspected, the law in all fifty states requires immediate referral of the student in question to an appropriate child protection agency. In no way should an educator question a child or a child's parents in regard to abuse or neglect without the involvement and support of the child protection agency.

Besides obvious physical abuse and neglect, educators will want to take into account periods of excessive fatigue or student strain and particularly when these symptoms occur. As with other identifying concerns, these symptoms may be more obvious on certain days than on others. These occurrences of fatigue, etc., may show a pattern, and it is the development of particular patterns of times of strain that should be observed the most. For children of alcoholic parents, these patterns are likely to reflect the occurrence of conflict within the home. For example, if an alcoholic parent is a chronic weekend drinker, every Monday may be manifested in the child falling asleep in class or being very listless. On Tuesdays through Thursdays the student may appear to be somewhat energetic, and on Friday exhibit high levels of tension at the thought of the coming weekend. Of course, different patterns can occur, and if your in-service program on children of alcoholic parents includes trained workers in alcoholism, they will be able to alert you to many symptoms of living in a family with alcoholism.

It is important that you be constantly alert to the needs of your students. If you are accurate in your observations, you will be able to be of considerable help to them in both how you behave and how you affect others in their actions. When talking with parents and professional colleagues, your accurate assessments of students may allow you to better inform them about what they can do and when referral is needed.

PART C

SUGGESTIONS FOR THERAPISTS AND PARENTS

7

Implications for Therapists

Therapists working with children of alcoholics should be especially concerned that their clients are able to establish positive relations with others and that they have confidence in their own abilities and worth. In order to help clients who have a parent who is an alcoholic to overcome personal inadequacies in these areas, three critical areas may need to be considered. These areas involve conditions for effecting positive relationships with others, ways of reducing feelings of powerlessness, and strategies for resolving conflict.*

---

*Of course, the professional therapist will assess the unique needs of their clients prior to attempting treatment. It is also recognized that the methods of treatment a therapist uses are the therapist's responsibility, that no particular type of therapy is suggested here. The purpose of the discussion in this chapter is to describe particular kinds of problems children of alcoholics suffer toward which therapists may need to be especially sensitive.

EFFECTIVE RELATIONSHIPS

One primary concern for the therapist should be the child's ability to develop and maintain quality primary relationships with others. It is quite likely that many children and adolescents who see a therapist will not have desirable relationships with their peers or adults. Many children of alcoholics have the problem of what some therapists refer to as being "socially disengaged;" in other words, their relationships with others are superficial and their contacts with others are often limited in number and intensity. When working with this problem, the therapist will need to be particularly sensitive to assessing the strengths and weaknesses of children of alcoholics as they are currently interacting with others. Whatever relationships therapists find, they will need to use them to build stronger as well as new social alignments for their clients.

Therapists have at their disposal many strategies for assessing the nature of a person's relationships with others. For example, one method of assessing the level of contact of influence others have on children of alcoholics is to use a sociogram. The sociogram is a method of constructing larger and larger circles, each representing different individuals or groups that influence the client with the client as the center of the circle. For example, the client represents the middle circle and the next circle represents "significant others" or those that have the most influence on the client. This circle usually includes the family members or close friends. As succeeding circles are added, each will have less influence on the client. In this manner, the therapist will be able to assess the people and the extent of their influence on the client.

Although the therapist can emphasize developing new relationships, it is usually necessary to examine existing ones with parents, as well as past relationships with parents. Clients may move from a relationship of confusion and love to one of frustration and bitterness. Helping children of alcoholics to interact more positively with their parents is critical. It is one relationship they can seldom escape no matter how old or even if they leave home.

However, the therapist need not be concerned with achieving sobriety in the client's parents or focusing on changing parents. The therapist who is only working with the client and not the client's family should be concerned with the physical and emotional survival of the client. A certain amount of the work of the therapist in this situation might be focused on "how to survive with an alcoholic parent." In this vain, getting clients to discuss their feelings about their situation and themselves may be more important than discussions that center on their alcoholic parents. The important thrust is to help the client of an alcoholic help him or herself to have more rewarding and healthy relationships at home with his or her parents and siblings, as well as with others outside the home. In other words, merely surviving in their home environment is not enough.

Other relationships the client of an alcoholic parent has with people outside of his or her family can also provide a support structure for not only the client's survival, but also for the client's growth as a person. Peers can provide many necessary friendships for healthy personal development. Therefore, the therapist may need to give considerable attention to helping some of their clients who are children of alcoholics with their peer relationships.

For those clients with only a few healthy peer relationships, the therapist may want to concentrate on developing various social skills. For example, some therapists may utilize tasks where the client is helped to attend a number of social functions whereby he or she meets new people. Those clients from alcoholic homes who have low feelings of self-esteem are prone to see themselves as uninteresting and feel that nobody likes to talk with them. If the therapist is able to help the client to develop adequate conceptions of self which are relevant to the various people with whom he or she comes in contact, then the foundation is laid for effective and needed primary relationships with others. The therapist will have to take a major step in helping his or her client survive and grow both outside and inside of their alcoholic home.

FEELINGS OF POWERLESSNESS

Children within an alcoholic home are likely to feel a strong sense of powerlessness. They are likely to see themselves as devoid of resources or ways of alleviating their parent's drinking or fighting. This felt loss of control can be carried over to other areas, including school. Most important, however, is that this sense of powerlessness can be felt to encompass every aspect of their lives. That is, they generally feel powerless over themselves.

In this situation, the therapist is faced with a "there is nothing I can do" attitude. Much of this feeling arises from a lack of an identity they value. Often children of alcoholics fail to see that their achievements can be, to a considerable extent, separate from those of their alcoholic parent. If they cannot influence their alcoholic parent, they wonder how they can help themselves. Therapists need to be sure that their clients establish a sense of valued identity and achievement independent of their identities as children of alcoholics. In this regard, conversations with the clients may need to be directed away from the home environment and more on the client and his or her aspirations and expectations outside of felt family needs.

One strategy in working with children of alcoholics is where the therapist helps the client to recognize that they cannot control the behavior of others whose effects they may have to endure. However, they can learn that they are able to control their own behavior, achievements, and feelings. To the extent that the therapist can help the client to develop a sense of control over his or her life, they facilitate the discovery for that client that he or she is an individual with appropriate and valuable feelings, attributes, and capabilities. In working through feelings of powerlessness, the development of a sense of valued identities can lead to internal resources for clients. These resources can enhance the abilities of the client for determining the outcomes of the behaviors of their alcoholic parents, even though they cannot control their parent's behavior.

In other words, it is important that children of alcoholics, like others, develop a sense of personal responsibility for much of what will happen to them. Unfortunately, all too often children of alcoholics conclude that their unhappiness or happiness is totally the result of others. Whether content or discontent, they perceive an inability to control their lives. The therapist in working with such clients may need to avoid having their clients shift from placing all responsibility for their problems on their parents to placing the responsibility for their happiness on them because they are their "therapist."

CONFLICT RESOLUTION

Most therapists believe that meeting the psychological needs of clients may require helping clients to resolve conflicts they may experience. One approach to conflict resolution focuses on three types of conflict that may occur. These are approach-approach conflict, avoidance-avoidance conflict, and approach-avoidance conflict.

Approach-Approach Conflict

Approach-approach conflict results when two goals are simultaneously desired, and to reach one goal will mean not achieving the other. It is common in the alcoholic home for the children to want to talk about their parent's drinking, but they also want to have good relationships with their parents. However, they fear that if they talk about their parent's drinking with their parents, their relationships with them will suffer. As a result, they may experience conflict within themselves. The force of external conditions appears to rule their lives. Mechanisms need to be developed for the expression of any such internal conflict. Without the outlet of expression, the client may be needlessly forced to endure excessive internal approach-approach conflict at the expense of many personal needs.

Avoidance-Avoidance Conflict

Avoidance-avoidance conflict is the typical circumstance of "you are damned if you do and damned if you don't." The child in an alcoholic home is likely to feel that

if he or she interferes with their parent's alcoholic behavior
that he or she will be sanctioned — in particular, that the
parent's love may be lost. Not to interfere, however, means
that the undesired drinking related behaviors of the parent
will continue. Another typical example in the family of
children of alcoholics is where the child is told the alcoholic
parent doesn't have a drinking problem, but they are also
told not to tell anyone about the parent's drinking habits.
If nothing is wrong, why not talk about it?

Approach-Avoidance Conflict

Another form of conflict is the approach-avoidance
type which is characterized by mixed feelings. A person is
attracted to an object, but is repulsed by some component
of it. The child of an alcoholic tends to love the alcoholic
parent rather intensely, while simultaniously hating the
drinking. The resolution of this type of conflict may be
the most challenging for a therapist. If the child is able to
overcome the distinction between the parent as an alcoholic
and as a parent with many qualities other than those of
being alcoholic, then the client may be able to see him or
herself with many attributes other than those of being a
member of an alcoholic home.

SUMMARY

Helping children of alcoholics to work through their feelings and establish effective relationships with others will be very helpful in overcoming the impact of an alcoholic parent. Moreover, the therapist will be helpful if he or she is able to assist such children in developing confidence in themselves. Clients need to believe that they can control how they feel about what is happening in their lives. They need to know that they can influence what is going to happen. If able to develop this self-confidence, the therapist's success will be far more reaching than that of just helping a client to survive while in an alcoholic home. The long-range effects may mean that the client will not become one of the forty to sixty percent of children of alcoholics who become alcoholics themselves.

8

Suggestions for Parents

Although it is desirable for alcoholic parents to stop drinking, it is not necessary for them to stop before they or their nonalcoholic spouses begin helping their children to overcome some of the problems caused by alcoholism. To wait might mean that their children are grown before sobriety occurs. Of course, much of what these parents can do to assist their children to overcome the consequences of their or their spouse's alcoholism will be dependent upon the conditions present in each family. Even so, there are a number of activities which are particularly appropriate for all parents.

The following suggestions are offered for both parents even though only one may be alcoholic:

- **Avoid pressuring your children, either verbally or with your actions, to take sides in conflicts you have with your spouse.**

Your children do not need nor do they usually want to take sides, but rather want you, their parents, to behave in ways that do not demand their siding with one or the other. If they are forced into taking one parent's side or another, even more problems are forced upon them. Further, pressure upon children to take sides in marital conflicts usually intensifies the conflict for both the husband and wife and the children.

- **Avoid using the opinions of your children about the use of alcohol or the alcoholic parent to get at the alcoholic.**

Using your children against your spouse is like taking sides and places them in a vulnerable position toward both you and your spouse. It may also cause your child to curtail a further sharing of feelings with you.

- **When the home situation is excessively disruptive or verbally abusive and your children go off to be alone, seek them out and comfort them.**

During family drinking episodes many children hide in the bathroom or their room because of fear or frustration. These episodes can be very upsetting. You should try to avoid letting your children go to sleep under upset conditions. If this occurs, talk with them at the first opportunity.

- **Avoid placing your oldest child in the position of being a confidant or surrogate parent to replace your spouse as parent.**

Making a surrogate parent of your child places too much strain on him or her and may also anger your spouse whose position your child is attempting to fulfill. Also, when the parent whose place they are taking resumes his or her duties, the child must revert to his or her original position in the family. This shifting of roles can lead your child to have feelings of inconsistency and to experience a serious personal problem.

- **Encourage and support your children to become involved in school and community activities.**

Your children, as others, need outlets and chances to develop needed relationships with others in activities outside of your home. Outside the home activities may help your child to develop understandings that he or she can accomplish many things on his or her own, that he or she can be independent of undesirable influences in your home.

- **Try to arrange times for your children to have their friends visit regularly.**

Your home should also be their home. Some alcoholics drink in patterns and provide some opportunity for normal family conditions. However, if your child has friends over and the alcoholic spouse is drinking, do not further embarrass your child or his or her friends by confronting the alcoholic. The time to talk with an alcoholic about his or her drinking is not when he or she is drinking.

● **Avoid exacting promises from your children that
they will never drink.**

If children of alcoholics decide to drink later in life,
this promise may cause unneeded guilt. It will also imply
to your child that he or she cannot handle alcohol. Many
alcoholics have high levels of guilt about their drinking.
Guilt may even increase their level of drinking because of
their perceived inability, often learned in the home, to control alcohol consumption.

● **Avoid constantly asking your children if you
should leave your spouse.**

Unless a separation has been decided upon, in which
case the children should be consulted, questioning your
children about when or if you should leave your spouse
only adds to the children's confusion of why you remain
together. This question is particularly inappropriate for
small children. They feel that parents are supposed to be
responsible and here a young child is being asked by a parent the most difficult of questions. Also, should a separation not occur, once you have raised these questions, your
children may live in fear that a separation will occur at any
time. This adds to your marital difficulties and to the personal problems of your children.

- **Educate yourself about alcoholism and community resources.**

It is difficult to help yourself or others unless you know what you are trying to work with. Much family frustration in alcoholic families arises from fears of unknown effects of drinking. Although you may not be able to get your spouse to stop drinking or to stop your own drinking, you can better prepare yourself and your children for survival.

- **Become involved in community resources or self-help groups for family members of alcoholics.**

Organizations such as Al-Anon and Alateen will greatly benefit the family. These groups provide for interaction and comradery with people in similar situations. Families of alcoholics need not be alone unless they choose to be.

- **If your alcoholic spouse seeks help, try to become involved as a family in the treatment process.**

Alcoholism affects the entire family and all will benefit from help. To allow the alcoholic to enter treatment alone is to deny a support structure for sobriety. Family members learn to adapt to the drinking alcoholic and need to learn to adapt to the recovering alcoholic. Once the alcoholic quits drinking, family life will change. The family — which includes, of course, your child — must be prepared to accept the alcoholic member back into the family physically and emotionally. Total recovery from alcoholism may require a total family effort.

Remember, if your children are to grow to have healthy and satisfying lives of their own, they will need the help of people and friends in their community, but most of all they will need you.

BUILDING SELF-ESTEEM IN A NEGATIVE WORLD

Practical Steps For Learning to Like Ourselves

A six-pamphlet series by

Earnie Larsen

Pamphlet 1: **"What Do I Believe About Myself?"**
On what is your self-esteem, self-confidence, and self-image based?

Pamphlet 2: **"The Shame Cycle"**
What is it? How is it operating in your life?

Pamphlet 3: **"The Steps for Building A Positive Self-Esteem"**
Are you willing to feel better about yourself?

Pamphlet 4: **"You, Too Can Have Healthy Relationships"**
Of course you can, if you are willing to make some changes.

Pamphlet 5: **"Learning to Manage Your Finances"**
Your self-esteem will skyrocket if you practice wise financial management.

Pamphlet 6: **"Finding Inner Peace"**
Your spirituality is at the core of your existence. Is it at peace?

E. Larsen Publishing
P.O. Box 33
Waconia, MN 55387-0033

APPENDIX A

RESOURCE MATERIALS

Suggested Books and Articles

A Selected Guide to Audio-Visual Materials on Alcohol and Alcoholism. National Institute on Alcohol Abuse and Alcoholism, 1975.

A Sensitive, Passionate Man. Pyramid, 1975.

Alateen — Hope for Children of Alcoholics. Al-Anon Family Group Headquarters, 1973.

Alcohol: Drink or Drug? Margaret O. Hyde, McGraw-Hill, 1974.

Alcohol Education Materials: An Annotated Bibliography. Gail G. Milgram, Rutgers Center of Alcohol Studies, 1975.

An Alcoholic in the Family. Lippincott, 1974.

"An Assessment of the Needs of and Resources for Children of Alcoholic Parents. Final Report." Booz, Allen and Hamilton, Inc., National Institute on Alcohol Abuse and Alcoholism, 1974.

Are You Driving Your Children to Drink? VanNos Reinhold, 1975.

"Children of Alcoholics: Observations in a Child Guidance Clinic." M. E. Chafetz, H. T. Blane, and M. J. Hill, *Quarterly Journal of Alcohol Studies,* 1971.

"Counseling Youth Whose Parents are Alcoholic: A Means to an End as Well as an End in Itself." W. R. Wier, *Journal of Alcohol Education,* 1970.

Dilemma of the Alcoholic Marriage. Al-Anon Family Group Headquarters, Inc., 1974.

Games Alcoholics Play: The Analysis of Life Scripts. Grove Press, 1971.

Living with Alcoholism. Beacon Press, 1968.

Love and Addiction. Stanton Peele, Signet, 1976.

Reaching Out: The Prevention of Drug Abuse Through Increased Human Interaction. Gerald Edwards, 37 Brompton Road, Garden City, New York 11530.

Society, Culture and Drinking Patterns. David Pittman and Charles Snyder, Southern Illinois University Press, 1962.

Struggles in an Alcoholic Family. Thomas, 1970.

The Alcoholic in Your Life. Warren Books, 1974.

"The Effect of Alcoholism on Children." Ruth Fox, National Council of Alcoholism, 1972.

The Forgotten Children. R. Margert Cork, Addiction Research Foundation, Ontario, 1969.

Values Clarification: A Handbook of Practical Strategies for Teachers and Students. Hart Publishing Co., 1972.

You and Your Alcoholic Parent. Associated Press, 1974.

Suggested Pamphlets

Titles: For Teenagers with an Alcoholic Parent

Facts About Alateen

Alateen Do's and Don'ts

A Guide for Sponsors of Alateen Groups

Al-Anon Faces Alcoholism

Living with an Alcoholic

The Dilemma of the Alcoholic Marriage

A Guide for the Family of an Alcoholic

Youth and the Alcoholic Parent

So You Love an Alcoholic

Source: Al-Anon Family Group Headquarters, Inc.
PO Box 182
Madison Square Station
New York, New York   10010

Titles: **Alcoholics Anonymous in Your Community**

              The Fellowship of Alcoholics Anonymous

              A. A. — 44 Questions and Answers

              Students' Guide to Alcoholics Anonymous

Source: Alcoholics Anonymous World Services, Inc.
              468 Park Avenue South
              New York, New York   10016

Title: **Alcoholism and the Family**

Source: Addiction Research Foundation
              33 Russell Street
              Toronto 4, Ontario

Title: **What Everyone Should Know about Alcoholism**

Source: A Scriptographic Booklet
              Channing L. Bete Co., Inc.
              Green Field, Massachusetts

Titles: **You and Your Alcoholic Parent**

              How to Help the Alcoholic

              Parent-Teenager Communication

              Combat Child Abuse and Neglect

              Alcoholics and Alcoholism

Source: Public Affairs Pamphlets
381 Park Avenue South
New York, New York   10016

Title: **Guide for the Family of the Alcoholic**

Source: Public Relations (D-1)
Kemper Insurance Companies
Long Grove, Illinois   60049

Title: **Alcoholism: A Family Illness**

Source: Rehabilitation Center
Lutheran General Hospital
Park Ridge, Illinois

Title: **Almost All You Ever Wanted to Know about Alcoholism, But Didn't Know How to Ask**

Source: AID
Box 212
Lansing, Michigan   48902

Suggested Films

Title: **Guidelines** (45 mins.)

Attitudes and values about alcohol and alcohol-ism are examined. Practical guidelines to help the alcoholic are explored.

Source: FMS Productions, Inc.
Los Angeles, California

Title: **The Summer We Moved to Elm Street** (30 mins.)

The family of an alcoholic is depicted through the eyes of a nine year old girl.

Source: McGraw-Hill Films
330 West 42nd Street
New York, New York 10036

Title: **Chalk Talk** (1 hour)

A discussion of alcohol and the body as well as various views on alcoholism.

Source: Department of the Navy
          U. S. Government Printing Office

Title: **Bitter Wind** (30 mins.)

          The story of a Navajo family and the attempts of
          a son to reunite his alcoholic family.

Source: Department of Audio-Visual Communications
          Brigham Young University
          Provo, Utah   84601

APPENDIX B

RESOURCE AGENCIES

Resource Agencies

Addiction Research Foundation
33 Russell Street
Toronto, Ontario, Canada

Al-Anon/Alateen Family Group Headquarters, Inc.
PO Box 182
Madison Square Station
New York, New York   10010

Alcoholics Anonymous World Services, Inc.
468 Park Avenue South
New York, New York   10016

Do It Now Foundation
National Media Center
PO Box 5115
Phoenix, Arizona   85010

Drug Abuse Council
1828 L Street, NW
Washington, DC   20036

Drug Enforcement Administration
1405 Eye Street, NW
Washington, DC   20537

MultiCultural Resource Center
8443 Crenshaw Boulevard
Inglewood, California   90305

National Center for Alcohol Education
1901 North Moore Street
Arlington, Virginia   22209

National Clearinghouse for Alcohol Information
PO Box 2345
Rockville, Maryland   20850

National Clearinghouse for Drug Abuse Information
PO Box 1908
Rockville, Maryland   20850

National Coordinating Council of Drug Education
1526 18th Street, NW
Washington, DC 20036

National Council on Alcoholism
2 Park Avenue
New York, New York   10016

National Institute on Alcohol Abuse and Alcoholism
5600 Fishers Lane
Rockville, Maryland   20852

National Institute of Drug Abuse
11400 Rockville Pike
Rockville, Maryland   20852

Rutgers Center of Alcohol Studies
Rutgers University
New Brunswick, New Jersey   08903

REFERENCES

Ackerman, R. J. "Socio-Cultural Aspects of Substance Abuse." *Competency-Based Training Manual for Substance Abuse Counselors,* Office of Substance Abuse Services, Department of Health, Michigan, 1978.

Alcohol Fact Sheet. National Council on Alcoholism, New York.

Berry, R. E. *The Economic Cost of Alcohol Abuse.* Free Press, New York, 1977.

Bosma, W. G. A. "Alcoholism and Teenagers." *Maryland State Medical Journal,* 1975.

Brookover, W., & Erickson, E. L. *Sociology of Education.* Dorsey Press, Illinois, 1975.

Chafetz, M. E., Blane, H. T., & Hill, M. J. "Children of Alcoholism: Observations in a Child Guidance Clinic." *Quarterly Journal of Alcohol Studies,* 1971.

Cork, M. R. *The Forgotten Children.* Addictive Research Foundation, Canada, 1969.

Craig, G. J. *Human Development.* Prentice-Hall, New Jersey, 1976.

Erickson, E. H. *Childhood and Society.* Norton, New York, 1963.

Fine, E., Yudin, L. W., Holmes, J., & Heinemann, S., "Behavior Disorders in Children with Parental Alcoholism." Paper presented at the Annual Meeting of the National Council on Alcoholism, Milwaukee, 1975.

Fontana, V. *Somewhere A Child is Crying.* Mentor, New York, 1976.

Forrest, G. G. *The Diagnosis and Treatment of Alcoholism.* Charles Thomas, New York, 1975.

Fox, R. "The Effect of Alcoholism on Children." National Council on Alcoholism, New York, 1972.

Hall, C. S., & Lindzey, G. *Theories of Personality.* Wiley, 1970.

Hecht, M. "A Cooperative Approach Towards Children from Alcoholic Families." *Elementary School Guidance and Counseling,* February, 1977.

Hindman, M. "Children of Alcoholic Parents." *Alcohol World Health & Research,* NIAAA, Winter, 1975-76.

Hornik, E. L. *You and Your Alcoholic Parent.* Association Press, New York, 1974.

Jackson, J. K. "The Adjustment of the Family to the Crises of Alcoholism." *Quarterly Journal of Studies on Alcohol, 1954.*

Jones, K. L., Smith, D. W., Ulleland, C., & Streissguth, A. P. "Pattern of Malformation in Offspring of Chronic Alcoholic Mothers." *Lancet,* 1973.

Lee, E. E. "Alcohol Education and the Elementary School Teacher." *The Journal of School Health,* 1976.

McKay, J. R., et al. "Juvenile Delinquency and Drinking Behavior." *Journal of Health and Human Behavior,* 1963.

Milgram, G. G. "Current Status and Problems of Alcohol Education in the Schools." *The Journal of School Health,* 1976.

Nylander, I. "Children of Alcoholic Fathers." *Acta Paediatrica,* 1960.

Oswald, R. M. *The Development and Function of Personality.* General Learning Press, 1976.

Papalia, D. E., & Olds, S. W. *Human Development.* McGraw-Hill, 1978.

Solomon, T. "History and Demography of Child Abuse." *Pediatrics,* 1973.

Weir, W. R. "Counseling Youth Whose Parents are Alcoholic: A Means to an End as Well as an End in Itself." *Journal of Alcohol Education,* 1970.

INDEX